The Way, The Truth, The Life

THE WAY, THE TRUTH, THE LIFE

A GUIDE FOR THE ROAD TO LIFE

P. D. BLACKWELL

The Way, The Truth, The Life: A Guide for the Road to Life

Copyright © 2026 All rights reserved

By P. D. Blackwell

ISBN: 978-1-7366096-5-1

No part of this book may be reproduced, or stored in a retrieval system, or transmitted in any form or by any means, electronic, mechanical, photocopying, recording, or otherwise, without express written permission of the publisher.

Contents

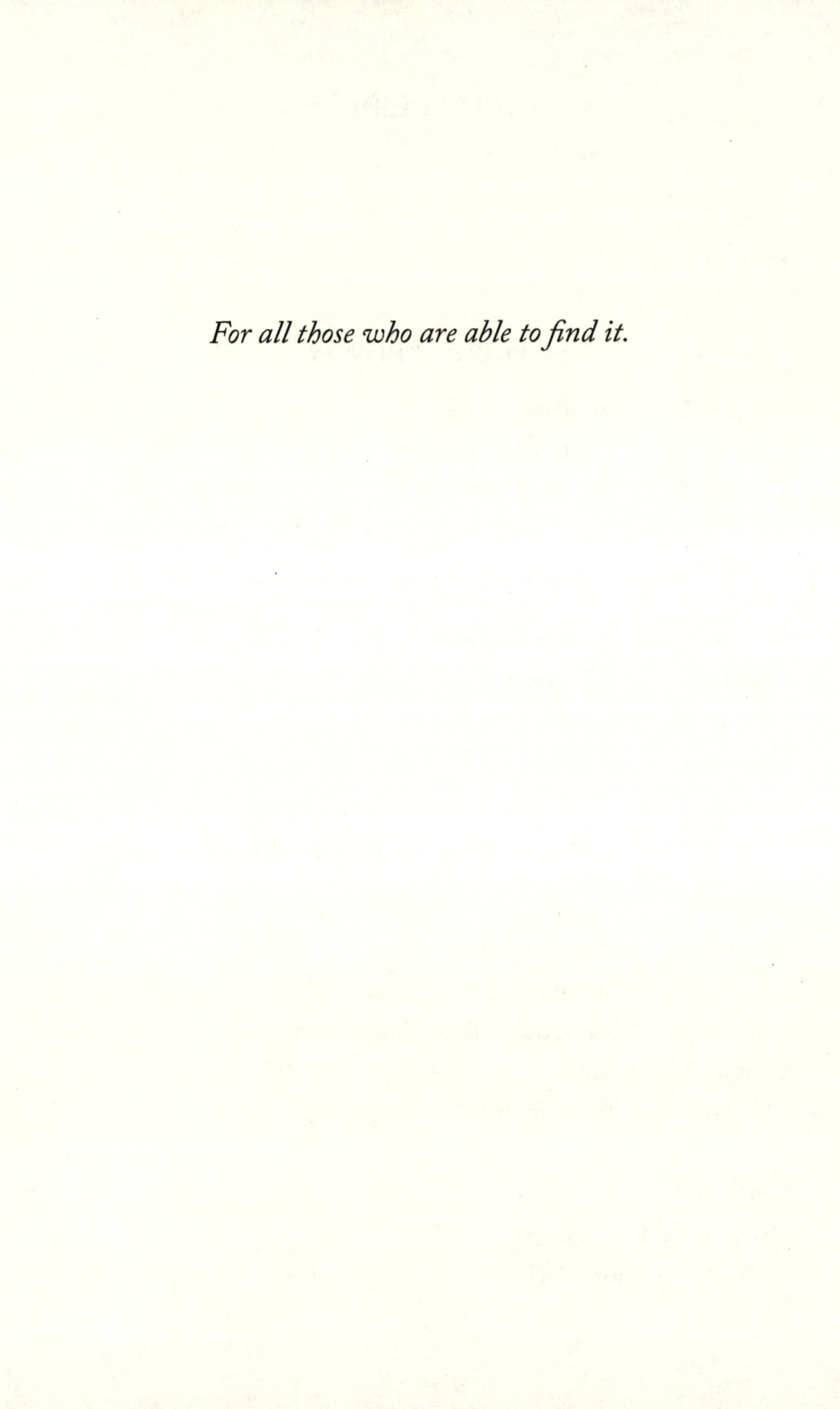

For all those who are able to find it.

List of Abbreviations

AMP - The Amplified Bible, ©1987, 2015, The Lockman Foundation.

ASV - American Standard Version, 1901, Public Domain.

BBE - Bible in Basic English, 1949, Cambridge Press, Public Domain.

BES - Brenton's English Septuagint, 1851, Public Domain.

CEV - Contemporary Engish Version, 1995, American Bible Society.

DRB - Douay-Rheims Bible, 1752, Public Domain.

ESV - English Standard Version, © 2016, Crossway Bibles.

GNB - Good News Bible, © 1992, American Bible Society.

ISV - International Standard Version, ©1996-2010, The ISV Foundation.

ISBE - International Standard Bible Encyclopedia, © 1980, Eerdmans.

JPS - Jewish Publication Society Old Testament, 1917, Public Domain.

KJV - King James Version, 1611, Public Domain.

LEB - Lexham English Bible, © 2012, Logos Research Systems, Inc.

LSB - Legacy Standard Bible, 2022, The Lockman Foundation.

NET - New English Translation, © 1996-2017, Biblical Studies Press.

NETS - New English Translation of the Septuagint, © 2007, Oxford.

NT - New Testament.

OT - Old Testament.

TGNT - The Greek New Testament, ©1983, United Bible Societies.

WEB - World English Bible, 2014, Public Domain.

WNT - The New Testament , 1937. C.B. Williams, Public Domain.

INTRODUCTION

In the fourteenth chapter of the Gospel of John, Jesus makes this statement:

> "I am the way, and the truth, and the life. No one comes to the Father except through me."—*John 14:6 LEB.*

This book will focus on what this statement means for everyone, not just what it implies about Jesus.

Our lives are not a predetermined, forced march to nowhere. We have options. Our free will is a gift from our Creator to use as we see fit. This book was written to help readers find the path to life, and successfully navigate the cramped road that leads to salvation.

Placed in the paradise of Eden, Adam and Eve would have been provided for by Yahweh, the Creator[1], the Self-Existing One[2], the Most High[3] among the Elohim[4], the Father of the Sons of God[5]. His power would have sustained them forever if they had demonstrated humility and recognized His sovereignty over all creation was not something to be ignored.

Just as a parent has the responsibility to guide their children, Yahweh's responsibility for humankind's growth never wavered. Just like human parents, Yahweh stood by his word when faced with disobedient offspring. Adam and Eve knew the options set before them, and the outcome for rejecting Yahweh's guidance. Because of willful disobedience, they had to suffer the consequences of their choices. The Most High's proclamations must always be fulfilled.

> Yahweh of hosts has sworn, saying, "Surely just as I have intended, so it shall be. And just as I have planned, it shall stand" . . . For Yahweh of hosts has planned, and who will frustrate it? And his hand is stretched out, and who will turn it back? — *Isaiah 14:24,27 LEB.*

> He has told you, O mortal, what is good, and what does Yahweh ask from you but to do justice, and to love kindness, and to walk humbly with your God? — *Micah 6:8 LEB.*

> The God who made the world and all the things in it . . . does not live in temples made by human hands, nor is he served by human hands as if he needed anything, because he himself gives to everyone life and breath and everything. — *Acts 17:24, 25 LEB.*

Yahweh's guidelines for a successful life were not a burden, nor were they an unrealistic restriction upon Adam and Eve. His laws were established to benefit his children.

> And Yahweh God commanded the man, saying, "From every tree of the garden you may freely eat, but from the tree of the knowledge of good and evil you shall not eat, for in the day that you eat from it you shall surely die." — *Genesis 2:16,17 LEB.*

> The woman said to the serpent, "From the fruit of the trees of the garden we may eat, but from the tree that is in the midst of the garden, God said, 'You shall not eat from it, nor shall you touch it, lest you die.'" — *Genesis 3:2,3 LEB.*

Adam and Eve's choices placed them, and their offspring, on a path separated from Yahweh. A way that leads only to death.

Because of his love, Yahweh made a way for Adam and Eve's offspring to avoid the ramifications of their parents' choices. That way was the promised Messiah, the one who would defeat the Nachash [6] (Serpent/Shining One) and restore paradise, as revealed to the Nachash in the first messianic prophecy:

> "And I will put enmity (open hostility) between you and the woman, And between your seed (offspring) and her seed (the Messiah); He shall [fatally] bruise your head, And you shall [only] bruise His heel." — *Genesis 3:15 AMP* (*See Galatians 4:4,5*).

The coming of the Messiah was Yahweh's solution to the travesty in Eden. Jesus is our model to follow, the only way to return to Yahweh free of condemnation. The following chapters will examine what that way implies for us and the obstacles that may impede our journey.

INTRODUCTION NOTES

1. Creator

Isaiah 40:28: "Have you not known, or have you not heard? Yahweh is the God of eternity, the creator of the ends of the earth! He is not faint, and he does not grow weary! There is no searching his understanding."

2. Self-Existing One

Exodus 3:14: "I am that I am" (KJV), is not the best translation of the Hebrew *ehaye asher ehaye*. "Ehaye" is the first-person imperfect form of the verb "hayah," defined as: to exist, that is, be or become, come to pass (see *The New Strong's Dictionary of Hebrew and Greek Words*. Nashville: Thomas Nelson, 1996.).

> In essence, the phrase reveals a God who is self-existent, self-defining, and actively present—transcending human categories while remaining intimately involved in his people's deliverance.
> - *Factbook*, Logos Bible Software, 2000-2026, Faithlife, LLC.

3. Most High

Gen 14:22: And Abram said to the king of Sodom, "I have raised my hand to Yahweh, God Most High, Maker of heaven and earth."

4. Elohim

Exodus 3:16: Go and gather the elders of Israel and say to them, "Yahweh, the God (elohim) of your ancestors, appeared to me, the God (elohim) of Abraham, Isaac, and Jacob."

5. Sons of God

The Sons of God are heavenly beings created before the creation of the Earth.

> "Where were you at my laying the foundation of the earth? Tell me, if you possess understanding. . . .When the morning stars were singing together and all the sons of God shouted for joy?" - Job 38:4,7.

> In several passages in the OT heavenly beings other than Yahweh are referred to by the expressions *bĕnê ʿelyôn* "children of Elyon" (Ps 82:6) and *bĕnê ʾēlîm* (Ps 29:1; 89:7) or *bĕnê (hā) ʾĕlōhîm* (Gen 6:2, 4; Job 1:6; 2:1; 38:7; and originally Deut 32:8 "children of God", "children of (the) gods" or "divine beings").

-Parker, S. B. *Sons of (The) God(S)*. In *Dictionary of Deities and Demons in the Bible*, edited by Karel van der Toorn, Bob Becking, and Pieter W. van der Horst. Leiden; Boston; Köln; Grand Rapids, MI; Cambridge: Brill; Eerdmans, 1999, 794.

6. Nachash (Serpent / Shining One)

I use the Hebrew word "Nachash" to name this individual because it is not a literal snake. Revelation 12:9 identifies the "dragon" as the "serpent, who is the Devil and the Satan."

This individual is referred to in Ezekiel as a Cherub (a Throne Guardian) at Ezekiel 28:12-19, and at Isaiah 14:12-15 as a "Shining One," the "morning star" who sought to "make myself like the Most High!" but was "brought down to the pit."

> The snake is an animal, but is like humans with respect to the power of language, and is like the gods with respect to secret knowledge. The snake's identity partakes and combines, in complex measure, characteristics of these three distinct categories of being . . . The choice of a venomous snake for this trickster figure seems predicated on traditional Near Eastern associations with the snake: associations with danger and death, with magic and secret knowledge, with rejuvenation and immortality. - R. S. Hendel, *Serpent*, in *Dictionary of Deities and Demons in the Bible*, ed. Karel van der Toorn, Bob Becking, and Pieter W. van der Horst (Leiden; Boston; Köln; Grand Rapids, MI; Cambridge: Brill; Eerdmans, 1999), 746–747.

Seraphim, who are also associated with Yahweh's throne, are described as serpents with wings. This could also be why the deceiver in Eden is called a "serpent."

> The Seraphim are now generally conceived as winged serpents with certain human attributes . . . It is generally taken as a derivative of the verb śārap, to "burn", "incinerate", "destroy". Since the verb is transitive, śārāp probably denotes an entity that annihilates by burning. [see Isaiah 6:2,3,6]. - T. N. D. Mettinger, *Seraphim*, in *Dictionary of Deities and Demons in the Bible*, ed. Karel van der Toorn, Bob Becking, and Pieter W. van der Horst (Leiden; Boston; Köln; Grand Rapids, MI; Cambridge: Brill; Eerdmans, 1999), 742,743.

PART ONE

THE WAY

Our lives begin on a broad road. At some point that road splits into different paths. It is then we must choose which path to take.

CHAPTER 1

THE PATHS OF REBELLION

We have choices to make from the day we are born. We have material needs and spiritual needs. The rift between humans and our Creator has hindered our spiritual relationship. Yahweh looks upon us as his wayward children, trapped in a lawless world, stifled by the tug of corrupt influences.

The First Rebellion

The first rebellion in Eden was prompted by willful disobedience to Yahweh's authority. Yes, Eve was deceived (2 Corinthians 11:3) but her deception was not blind. She knew the restrictions put upon her and Adam were for their benefit; a boundary set to prevent them from dying. (Genesis 3:2,3). The words spoken by the Nachash (Serpent/Shining One), caused her to focus on personal desire, which drew her mind away from the reality of Yahweh's warning, into a mindset that whirled with emotion; an understanding she and Adam could become like God, and choose for themselves the path they should take (Genesis 3:4,5). Fueled by this selfish desire, Eve left the comfort and protection provided by Yahweh and stepped onto a path of willful lawlessness, abandoning her relationship with her Creator. Adam, neither deceived nor ignorant of the consequences, followed Eve into lawlessness. (Genesis 3:6; 1 Corinthians 15:22).

The Second Rebellion

The second rebellion is revealed in Genesis, chapter 6.

> And it happened that, when humankind began to multiply on the face of the ground, daughters were born to them. Then the sons of God saw the daughters of humankind, that they were beautiful. And they took for themselves wives from all that they chose. And Yahweh said, "My Spirit shall not abide with humankind forever in that he is also flesh. And his days shall be one hundred and twenty years." The Nephilim were upon the earth in those days, and also afterward, when the sons of God went into the daughters of humankind, and they bore children to them. These were the mighty warriors that were from ancient times, men of renown. — *Genesis 6:1-4. LEB.*

This rebellion of the Sons of God, (běnê hā ʾĕlōhim, Genesis 6:2), was another rejection of Yahweh's authority and the standards he set for all his creation. The Sons of God are heavenly beings, creatures created to live in the spirit realm. They witnessed the creation of the Earth (Job 38:4-7). They were never made to cohabit with humans and produce offspring via human females.

> You also know that the angels who did not keep within their proper domain but abandoned their own place of residence, he has kept in eternal chains in

> utter darkness, locked up for the judgment of the great Day. —*Jude 1:6 NET.*

> For if God did not spare the angels who sinned, but held them captive in Tartarus with chains of darkness and handed them over to be kept for judgment. —*2 Peter 2:4 NET.*

The rebellion of the Sons of God increased evil upon the world, as the heavenly beings influenced human civilization and produced hybrid offspring called Nephilim. (Genesis 6:4). This corruption of flesh was in response to the first prophecy about the Messiah.

> Yahweh God said to the serpent, "Because you have done this, you are cursed above all livestock, and above every animal of the field. You shall go on your belly and you shall eat dust all the days of your life. I will put hostility between you and the woman, and between your offspring and her offspring. He will bruise your head, and you will bruise his heel." —*Genesis 3:14,15 WEB.*

This prophecy about the Messiah, who would be a "seed" or "offspring" of the woman; a human being who would "bruise" the heavenly being called Nachash (Serpent/Shining One) by striking his "head," (a more significant blow than being struck on the heel), was Yahweh's response to the sin encouraged by the Nachash. The way to forestall the prophecy would be to prevent the Messiah from being born. One way to do that would be to corrupt all human flesh, and so the hybrid agenda began. Heavenly beings who sided with the Nachash came to the Earth, took wives, and their seed produced

Nephilim, which corrupted all flesh on the Earth. (Genesis 6:4-7,12).

This rebellion led to the Great Flood (Genesis 6:13; 7:21-24).

The Third Rebellion

The third rebellion happened after the Great Flood. Once the waters receded and Noah left the ark, Yahweh repeated twice the command he had given Adam:

> Then God blessed Noah and his sons and said to them, "Be fruitful and multiply and fill the earth."— *Genesis 9:1 LEB.*

> "And you, be fruitful and multiply, swarm on the earth and multiply in it."— *Genesis 9:7 LEB.*

It was always Yahweh's intention to have the Earth filled with living creatures, both human and animal. Yet, Noah's descendants chose a different path. They decided to congregate in one place to "make a name" for themselves (Genesis 11:1-4). This led to the Babel rebellion, and caused Yahweh to confuse human languages so that the people would scatter and "fill the Earth."

> Then Yahweh came down to see the city and the tower that humankind was building. And Yahweh said, "Behold, they are one people with one language, and this is only the beginning of what they will do. So now nothing that they intend to do will be impossible for them. Come, let us go down and confuse their language there, so that they will not understand each

> other's language." So Yahweh scattered them from there over the face of the whole earth, and they stopped building the city. Therefore its name was called Babel, for there Yahweh confused the language of the whole earth, and there Yahweh scattered them over the face of the whole earth. — *Genesis 11:5-9 LEB.*

This third rebellion revealed to Yahweh that humans, as a united group, would not follow his will; they would pursue their own will. Because of this, He withdrew his influence over them and placed them under the oversight of the Sons of God. This is not mentioned in Genesis, but is revealed in Deuteronomy.

> When the Most High apportioned the nations, at his dividing up of the sons of humankind, he fixed the boundaries of the peoples, according to the number of the sons of God. — *Deuteronomy 32:8 LEB.*

Bibles based on the *Masoretic Text* translate this verse, "according to the number of the children of Israel." The *Masoretic Text* was compiled in the Middle Ages and received its final form in the 10th-century C.E. under Aaron Ben Asher of the Tiberian Masoretes (See: *Textual Criticism of the Hebrew Bible* by Emanuel Tov). Since "Israel" did not exist at the time of the scattering at Babel, the "children of Israel" is an obvious corruption of the text. This was proven after the Dead Sea Scroll 4Q37 was discovered to have "according to the sons of God," and was dated to 50 C.E.. The Septuagint, the Greek translation of the Hebrew text, whose origins date between 280 B.C.E. and 150 B.C.E., agrees with the Dead Sea Scroll.

> When the Most High divided the nations, when he separated the sons of Adam, he set the bounds of the nations according to the number of the angels of God. — *Deuteronomy 32:8 - BES.*

> When the Most High was appointing nations, as he scattered Adam's sons, he fixed the boundaries of nations according to the number of divine sons. — *Deuteronomy 32:8 NETS.*

These earlier texts are more in harmony with other scriptures and support the fourth rebellion between the Spiritual Principalities and Yahweh, established by the remaining text of Genesis and the rest of the books of the Old Testament.

The Fourth Rebellion

This fourth rebellion is not between Yahweh and humans; it is between Yahweh and the Sons of God who rule the Spiritual Principalities that have oversight of the earthly nations. Yahweh put humans under the oversight of the Sons of God because he knew Adam's offspring still needed guidance, and moving forward, Yahweh was going to focus on a new nation he would make from Abram, who became Abraham.

Unfortunately, the Sons of God did not handle their new obligations well. They received chastisement from Yahweh and will experience the ultimate penalty of death as recorded in Psalm 82.

> God stands in the divine assembly;
> He administers judgment in the midst of the gods.
> "How long will you judge unjustly

and show favoritism to the wicked?
Judge on behalf of the helpless and the orphan;
provide justice to the afflicted and the poor.
Rescue the helpless and the needy;
deliver them from the hand of the wicked."
They do not know or consider.
They go about in the darkness,
so that all the foundations of the earth are shaken.
I have said, "You are gods,
and sons of the Most High, all of you.
However, you will die like men,
and you will fall like one of the princes."
Rise up, O God, judge the earth,
because you shall inherit all the nations.
— *Psalm 82:1-15 LEB.*

Some may argue that the "gods" mentioned in this psalm are human judges. That opinion does not agree with the context. This is a "divine assembly," a gathering of the heavenly Elohim with God (Yahweh) in their midst. These Sons of the Most High are divine (heavenly) beings who have been put in charge of the earthly nations, and they have allowed wickedness to thrive. They will "die like men" because they are not men; they are Elohim (heavenly beings) who have tossed aside their responsibilities and been proven corrupt.

These divine Sons of God are the "spiritual forces of wickedness in the heavenly places" mentioned by the Apostle Paul in his letter to the Ephesians:

> Put on the full armor of God, so that you may be able to stand against the stratagems of the devil, because our struggle is not against blood and flesh, but against

> the rulers, against the authorities, against the world rulers of this darkness, against the spiritual forces of wickedness in the heavenly places. — *Ephesians 6:11,12. LEB.*

We are told about two of these divine sons at Daniel 10:13, the Prince of Persia, and at Daniel 10:20, the Prince of Yavan (Greece). We know these "princes" must be heavenly beings because a human prince of Persia could not stop an angel from reaching Daniel, and even if another human prince of Greece came to help a human prince of Persia, they would not succeed against an angel. These "princes" were so powerful that the Archangel Michael had to help the unnamed message-bearer reach Daniel (Daniel 10:21).

The Impact Upon Civilization

These four rebellions were the result of free will applied with selfish intent. That is the negative aspect of free will: the ability to choose despite bad consequences. For free will to be successful, it must allow choices free of mandates. Yahweh wants His creation to follow His guidance by choice, not because of intimidation or programmed instinct. This is the hope of all good parents: children who grow with wisdom and the fortitude to choose the good path, despite pressure to sidestep to the path that leads to immediate gratification but ends with bad consequences.

The failure of the Sons of God to pursue Yahweh's will in all things set the stage for the rest of the Old and New Testaments. This conflict overshadows everything that has occurred since Babel. The Messiah came not just for the salvation of Adam's offspring, but for the restoration of Yahweh's will over all creation.

For look! I am about to create new heavens and a new earth, and the former things shall not be remembered, and they shall not come to mind. —*Isaiah 65:17 LEB.*

But the things which God foretold through the mouth of all the prophets, that his Christ would suffer, he has fulfilled in this way. Therefore repent and turn back, so that your sins may be blotted out, so that times of refreshing may come from the presence of the Lord, and he may send the Christ appointed for you—Jesus, whom heaven must receive until the times of the restoration of all things, about which God spoke through the mouth of his holy prophets from earliest times. —*Acts 3:18-21 LEB.*

I consider that what we suffer at this present time cannot be compared at all with the glory that is going to be revealed to us. All of creation waits with eager longing for God to reveal his children. For creation was condemned to lose its purpose, not of its own will, but because God willed it to be so. Yet there was the hope that creation itself would one day be set free from its slavery to decay and would share the glorious freedom of the children of God. — *Romans 8:18-21 GNB.*

Chapter 2

The Road to Perdition

Parents rule their household. Children grow under the guidelines set by the parents. If the children ignore the parents' authority, their status within the household will change. If the behavior of the children becomes severe beyond correction, the only option is to remove them from the household.

Yahweh, as a good parent, set boundaries and explained the ramifications of stepping outside prescribed limits. He established guidelines for the success of his creation. All of the lifeforms on Earth were created for a specific reason. The Earth's environment lives and breathes with lifeforms in diverse niches, who all impact the ecosystem on different levels. Every creature is an important part of the ecosystem of life, from the microscopic amoeba to the largest wild beasts on land and in the sea. Only humans were given oversight of all animals in their environment (Genesis 1:26, 27), but under the sovereignty of Yahweh, the Creator.

The four rebellions discussed in the last chapter were the outgrowth of the same problem: the desire to be free from Yahweh's sovereignty. This ability to choose is the foundation of free will. No human or heavenly being is forced to follow Yahweh's will, but all persons will be accountable for the path they take. We all reap what we sow.

> Do not be deceived. God will not be made a fool. For a person will reap what he sows. — *Galatians 6:7 NET.*

With the law established, and a future under Yahweh's guidance a guaranteed paradise, why would anyone seek their own authority and reject Yahweh's sovereignty? The reason is selfish desire: the pride of personal fulfillment.

The created being who exemplifies this attitude is the one called the Devil and the Satan. These two terms are not proper names. They are titles that reveal this person's character.

The word "Satan" means "adversary." This title stems from actions taken in Eden by the one called "Nahcash" (Serpent/Shining One), who is later identified as "the Devil" and "the Satan."

> Καὶ [And] ἐβλήθη [thrown] ὁ [the] δράκων [dragon] ὁ [the] μέγας, [great,] ὁ [the] ὄφις [serpent] ὁ [the] ἀρχαῖος, [ancient,] ὁ [who] καλούμενος [is called] Διάβολος [Devil] καὶ [and] ὁ [the] Σατανᾶς. [Satan]. — *Revelation 12:9 TGNT .*

> Καὶ [And] ἐκράτησεν [he seized] τὸν [the] δράκοντα, [dragon], ὁ [the] ὄφις [serpent] ὁ [the] ἀρχαῖος, [ancient], ὅς [who] ἐστιν [is] Διάβολος [Devil] καὶ [and] ὁ [the] Σατανᾶς. [Satan]. — *Revelation 20:2 TGNT.*

The word "Devil" is a rendering of the Greek word διάβολος (diabŏlŏs), and describes someone slanderous and defamatory; a person who uses lies to malign others. This attitude grew within a once trusted Son of God and gave birth to rebellion.

The prophet Ezekiel tells us a lament about the king of Tyre (Ezekiel 28:1-19), who proves to be a reflection of the spiritual Son of God who became the Devil and the Satan. The King's attitude was influenced by the Devil the same way Eve was influenced in Eden. All offspring of Adam and Eve are born under the power of the evil one, and many, like the king of Tyre, align their minds with the Devil and oppose Yahweh's will.

> We know that we are from God, and the whole world lies in the power of the evil one. - *1 John 5:19 LEB.*

> And you, although you were dead in your trespasses and sins, in which you formerly walked according to the course of this world, according to the ruler of the authority of the air, the spirit now working in the sons of disobedience. — *Ephesian 2:1,2 LEB.*

Ezekiel's words begin with condemnation for the human king, but then (beginning in verse 12) his focus turns to the spiritual rebel, the spirit who became the Adversary, the ruler of the authority of the air, who is influencing the human king.

> "Son of man, raise a lament over the king of Tyre." — *Ezekiel 28:12. LEB.*

We naturally think of the human king as we read this quotation from Ezekiel, but based on the content of the following message, and the biblical understanding that the rulers behind all nations are spiritual beings, as revealed in Daniel 10:13-20 (Prince of Persia and Prince of Greece), and the admonition by Paul in Ephesians 6:12 that "our struggle is not against blood and flesh," but against, "the spiritual forces of wickedness in the heavenly places," the identity of the "king" shifts to the real power behind the leadership of Tyre.

> Son of man, raise a lament over the king of Tyre, and you must say to him, 'Thus says the Lord Yahweh: "You were a perfect model of an example, full of wisdom and perfect of beauty.
> "You were in Eden, the garden of God, and every precious stone was your adornment: carnelian, topaz and moonstone, turquoise, onyx and jasper, sapphire, malachite and emerald. And gold was the craftsmanship of your settings and your mountings in you; on the day when you were created they were prepared.
> "You were an anointed guardian cherub, and I placed you on God's holy mountain; you walked in the midst of stones of fire. You were blameless in your ways from the day when you were created, until wickedness was found in you."' — *Ezekiel 28:12-15 LEB.*

The term "Cherub" (singular) or "Cherubim" (plural) is a Hebrew term for a throne guardian.

> While the biblical cherubim sometimes appear as guardians of the sacred tree (1 Kgs 6:29–35; Ezek 41:18–25) or of the garden of Eden (Gen 3:24; Ezek 28:14, 16), the most important function is that of bearers of →Yahweh's throne, cf. [compare] Ezek 10:20 and the divine epithet *yōšēb hakkĕrûbim*, "he who is enthroned on the cherubim", applied to Yahweh already at Shilo (1 Sam 4:4; cf. 2 Sam 6:2; Isa

> 37:16 etc.). — T. N. D. Mettinger, *Cherubim*, in *Dictionary of Deities and Demons in the Bible*, ed. Karel van der Toorn, Bob Becking, and Pieter W. van der Horst (Leiden; Boston; Köln; Grand Rapids, MI; Cambridge: Brill; Eerdmans, 1999), pg. 189–190.

As we continue in Ezekiel 28, we are told how this cherub fell from grace and the ultimate end of his existence; his unavoidable future.

> In the abundance of your trading, they filled the midst of you with violence, and you sinned; and I cast you as a profane thing from the mountain of God, and I expelled you, the guardian cherub, from the midst of the stones of fire. Your heart was proud because of your beauty; you ruined your wisdom because of your splendor. I threw you on the ground before kings; I have exposed you for viewing.
>
> From the abundance of your iniquities in the dishonesty of your trading, I profaned your sanctuaries, and I brought fire from your midst; it consumed you, and I have turned you to ashes on the earth before the eyes of everyone who sees you. All who know you among the peoples are appalled over you; you have become as horrors, and you shall cease to exist forever. — *Ezekiel 28:16-19 LEB.*

The term "cease to exist" in Ezekiel 28:19 is taken from the Hebrew *ah'-yin,* and has the meaning: to *be nothing,* or *not exist*; a *non-entity.* (*The New Strong's Dictionary of Hebrew and Greek Words.*

Nashville: Thomas Nelson, 1996). This outcome implies complete destruction, or the state of perdition.

> *Perdition* began life as a word meaning "utter destruction"; that sense is now archaic, but it provides a clue about the origin of the word. "Perdition" was borrowed into English in the 14th-century from Anglo-French *perdiciun* and ultimately derives from the Latin verb *perdere,* meaning "to destroy." — *Merriam-Webster Dictionary, Online Edition* https://www.merriam-webster.com/dictionary/perdition.

The word "perdition" has taken on a different meaning in this 21st-century as a place (or a spiritual dimension) of punishment for the wicked, often synonymous with "hell." (see Merriam-Webster Dictionary). This is due to changes in theological perspectives. The word "perdition" was used by the *King James* translators for the Greek word ἀπώλεια (apōleia), a derivative of ἀπόλλυμι (apŏllumi); to *destroy* fully. The altered theological meaning of "perdition" since the 17th-century, has caused some modern English translators to return to the original meaning of the Greek, and use "destruction" as the translation. (See John 17:12, Philippians 1:28, 2 Thessalonians 2:3, Revelation 17:8, 11).

The original *King James* use of "perdition" implied the punishment of total destruction, an everlasting non-existence. That is the way Yahweh removes those who rebel against His sovereignty.

Just as a parent would evict children who promote wickedness in their home, Yahweh will evict everyone from his kingdom who does not accept his rightful sovereignty. This is not a decision made out of anger or jealousy. It is a judicial determination based on the actions and heart of the person punished.

Since Yahweh is not evil, he will not torture unrepentant individuals for eternity (James 1:13). His kingdom encompasses the entire physical and spiritual universe, where there will no longer be a place for anyone opposed to his will. The best and simplest course of action is to evict the wicked from his kingdom so they can never harm anyone again. Yahweh will be done with them forever, because they will exist no more.

> And I heard a loud voice from the throne saying, "Behold, the dwelling of God is with humanity, and he will take up residence with them, and they will be his people, and God himself will be with them. And he will wipe away every tear from their eyes, and death will not exist any longer, and mourning or wailing or pain will not exist any longer. The former things have passed away." — *Revelation 21:3.4 LEB.*

> When the wicked flourish like grass and all the workers of evil blossom, it is so they can be destroyed forever. — *Psalm 92:7 LEB.*

> Observe the blameless and look at the upright, for there is a future for a man of peace. But transgressors shall be destroyed altogether. The future of the wicked shall be cut off. — *Psalm 37:37,38 LEB.*

CHAPTER 3

THE ROAD TO LIFE

The road to life is narrow and full of obstacles.

> Enter through the narrow gate, because broad is the gate and spacious is the road that leads to destruction, and there are many who enter through it, because narrow is the gate and constricted is the road that leads to life, and there are few who find it! — *Matthew 7:13 LEB.*

> Exert every effort to enter through the narrow door, because many, I tell you, will try to enter and will not be able to. — *Luke 13:24 NET.*

The word translated "exert every effort" at Luke 13:24 in the *New English Translation*, is the Greek verb ἀγωνίζεσθε (agōnidzĕsthĕ), the present, either middle or passive, imperative, second person, plural of ἀγωνίζομαι (agōnidzŏmai): to struggle; literally, to compete for a prize; figuratively, to contend with an adversary; or generally, to endeavor to accomplish something: fight, labor fervently, strive. (See: *The New Strong's Dictionary of Hebrew and Greek Words,* Nashville: Thomas Nelson, 1996). This implies a doorway that takes effort to negotiate.

> The word [agōnidzŏmai] is taken from the Grecian games. In their races, and wrestlings, and various athletic exercises, they "strove or agonized," or put forth all their powers to gain the victory. — Albert Barnes, *Notes on the Bible,* Luke 13:24, Published in 1847-1885.

Without effort, nothing is gained. The road to life must be found, and that discovery can only be made by acquiring knowledge.

> For if you cry out for understanding, if you lift your voice for insight, if you seek her like silver and search her out like treasure, then you will understand the fear of Yahweh, and the knowledge of God you will find. For Yahweh will give wisdom; from his mouth come knowledge and understanding. — *Proverbs 2: 3-6 LEB.*

Finding the road is only the beginning. Staying on the road is the most difficult part of the journey.

> The recommendation of the broad way is the ease with which it is trodden and the abundance of company to be found in it. It is sailing with a fair wind and a favorable tide . . . The one disadvantage of this course is its end—it "[leads] to destruction."
> As to the other way, the disadvantage of it lies in its narrowness and solicitude. Its very first step involves a revolution in all our purposes and plans for life, and a surrender of all that is dear to natural inclination, while all that follows is but a repetition of the first great act of self-sacrifice. No wonder, then, that few find and few are found in it. But it has one

> advantage—it "[leads] unto life." — *Commentary Critical and Explanatory on the Whole Bible*, Jamieson, Fausset, and Brown, vol. 2 (Oak Harbor, WA: Logos Research Systems, Inc., 1997), page 30.

> Jesus explains that the way to God's kingdom is like a road less traveled. The concept of two ways—one leading to life and the other to destruction—appears in the Hebrew Bible, Graeco-Roman literature, and the Jewish writings from the Dead Sea Scrolls (ca. 250 BC–50 AD). — John D. Barry et al., *Faithlife Study Bible* (Bellingham, WA: Lexham Press, 2012, 2016), Mt 7:13–14.

Once the narrow gate is behind us, the narrow road will have many obstacles in our path we may have never foreseen. This requires humility and the surrender of all lawless desires that can pull us away from a meaningful relationship with God. The struggle is not the abandonment of freedom, for "the truth will set you free" (John 8:32). It is the abandonment of worldly desires and perspectives that complicate and degrade our lives, while impeding the discovery of truth.

Spiritual understanding takes time. Over time our knowledge will grow and our progress will be more evident. The road to life gets easier as we progress, but takes constant effort to reach our ultimate goal.

> Therefore, since we are surrounded by so great a cloud of witnesses [*who by faith have testified to the truth of God's absolute faithfulness*], stripping off every unnecessary weight and the sin which so easily *and* cleverly entangles us, let us run with endurance *and*

> active persistence the race that is set before us. — *Hebrews 12:1 AMP.*

The "way" to the road where the race for life happens is through Jesus. This means there is no other "way" to life. We can only approach God through his son.

> For there is one God and one mediator between God and human beings, the man Christ Jesus. — *1 Timothy 2:5 LEB.*

The only way to pass the obstacles on the road to life is by aligning our will with God's will.

> Stop living in accordance with the customs of this world, but by the new ideals that mold your minds continue to transform yourselves, so as to find and follow God's will; that is, what is good, well-pleasing to Him, and perfect. — *Romans 12:2 WNT.*

> For you have need of endurance, in order that after you have done the will of God, you may receive what was promised. — *Hebrews 10:36 LEB.*

> Therefore, because Christ suffered in the flesh, you also equip yourselves with the same way of thinking, because the one who has suffered in the flesh has ceased from sin, in order to live the remaining time in the flesh no longer for human desires, but for the will of God . . . So then, also those who suffer according to the will of God must entrust their souls to a faithful Creator in doing good.— *1 Peter 4:1,2,19 LEB.*

PART TWO

THE TRUTH

Some people say truth is relative, that each of us is bound by our own truth. While our perspectives are bound by what we have been taught and experienced, we can break through those barriers if our minds are open to new ideas. With the influx of new information, our reason can decipher between fact and fiction. From that will come wisdom, and a truth based on reality, not the tradition of fools.

Chapter 4

Facts Build Reality

Truth is the summation of facts when speaking about a narrow set of data, like simple mathematic equations: $1 + 1 = 2$, $6 \div 3 = 2$, or the sum of the more complex: (x^2 + 4x + 7 = 0). Mathematical "proofs" are steadfast summations when correct, as are all results of a correct analysis of both numerical and empirical data.

Facts of history are another matter. Truthful history is the summation of evidence. The strength of the evidence determines the correctness of every historical event. The correctness of a stated history can change if the evidence changes. One example of this is the city of Troy.

> Troy is the name of the Bronze Age city attacked in the Trojan War, a popular story in the mythology of ancient Greece, and the name given to the archaeological site in the north-west of Asia Minor (now Turkey), which has revealed a large and prosperous city occupied over millennia. There has been much scholarly debate as to whether mythical Troy actually existed, and if so, whether the archaeological site was the same city; however, it is now almost universally accepted that the

> archaeological excavations have revealed the city of Homer's *Iliad.* —*World History Encyclopedia* (online edition). https://www.worldhistory.org/troy/

Truth in the Bible regarding history is no different from secular historical facts; the evidence from archaeological discoveries has proven the Bible to be historically accurate, where it was once considered myth.

> For centuries, skeptics have questioned the historical reliability of biblical narratives. Today, archeology offers tangible connections to these ancient texts. Modern excavations across the Middle East have uncovered artifacts that align with scriptural accounts, from minor details to major historical events . . . Each discovery adds context and credibility to the scriptural narrative. What makes recent findings especially significant is how they've settled long-standing scholarly debates about biblical chronology and the existence of key figures. The pace of discovery shows no signs of slowing down, with new technologies revealing previously invisible details. —*Science Sensei,* https://sciencesensei.com/35-archaeological-finds-that-verify-christian-scriptures/

While historical facts are important, the Bible contains more than historical events. It is a record of Yahweh's guidance for successful human civilization, and reveals the motivation behind His intention for all life, both on Earth and in the unseen spiritual realm.

Many of the proclamations in scripture about future events have been fulfilled and have been recorded as facts of history by archeology. As for Yahweh's intentions, the events recorded in scripture reveal His personality and His motivation behind all His actions. The prophetic words that have yet to be fulfilled, like the promise of a return to paradise, must be analyzed from an internal perspective. In other words, there must be consistency throughout the scriptures; the Bible must be internally harmonious, true to itself. Any deviation would make Yahweh a liar. To do this successfully, we must review everything in context. This means not just analyzing what was said, but also who said it, and in what time period they said it. The Scriptures were not written to us. They were written to a people who lived at a different time in a different culture, so we must adopt their perspective to understand the intent behind what was written.

An example of apparent inconsistency is the difference between genealogies in the Old Testament. Upon further examination, we find valid evidence that explains why differences are found.

> Two types of genealogies are attested in the Bible:
> 1. Linear, where the genealogy records one individual for each generation (e.g., Genesis 5)
> 2. Segmented, where the genealogy divides across multiple individuals through some or all of the generations it records (e.g., Genesis 10).
> Genealogies are rarely included in biblical narrative purely to preserve objective historical data. They are thus not always comprehensive, omitting some generations because they were either superfluous to the author's aim or disrupted the literary format the author was using. Omitting generations in a

> genealogy is known as "telescoping" and is evident in a number of biblical genealogies . . . This phenomenon is also evident in non-biblical genealogies such as the *Abydos King List* from Egypt, which omits three groups of kings (the Ninth to early Eleventh Dynasties, the Thirteenth to Seventeenth Dynasties, and the Amarna pharaohs) at three separate points in an otherwise continuous series (Kitchen, *Ancient Orient*, 38).
>
> Telescoping alone does not undermine the historical veracity of any particular genealogy. Since the function was not to provide a comprehensive lineage but rather a genealogical link between the beginning and end, to treat all biblical genealogies as comprehensive records is to misread them. . . Genealogies can serve a number of functions depending upon their context. In the Bible, however, genealogies never appear primarily to preserve historical detail—they invariably serve other functions. — *Genealogy, The Lexham Bible Dictionary,* Lexham Press, 2016.

While the subject of genealogy is extensive and beyond the scope of this book, it serves as an example of what may appear simple, but was intended by the author differently than how it is initially perceived by modern readers.

This difference in perspective is the main cause of confusion when attempting to understand the biblical narrative. We will discuss perspective further in the following section. For now, please contemplate the following scriptures.

> My son, if you will receive my words, and store up my commandments within you; So as to turn your ear to wisdom, and apply your heart to understanding; Yes, if you call out for discernment, and lift up your voice for understanding; If you seek her as silver, and search for her as for hidden treasures: then you will understand the fear of Yahweh, and find the knowledge of God. For Yahweh gives wisdom. Out of his mouth comes knowledge and understanding.
> — *Proverbs 2: 1-6 LEB.*

Our effort to dig for the truth will be rewarded with understanding that will build up our faith and help us find the narrow road to life.

> I have complete confidence in the gospel; it is God's power to save all who believe, first the Jews and also the Gentiles. For the gospel reveals how God puts people right with himself: it is through faith from beginning to end. As the scripture says, "The person who is put right with God through faith shall live"
> — *Romans 1:16.17 GNB.*

CHAPTER 5

A PERSONAL REALITY

We see through our own unique perspectives. This is true physically as well as spiritually. If our worldview is based solely on secular data, our vision will be limited, and the spiritual perspective we need to see God will be blocked. To adopt a biblical worldview our perspective must change. This does not mean altering our entire lives. It means adjusting our perception; opening our eyes to other possibilities.

> Perspective is not just a way of looking — it's a way of living. It helps us pause, reinterpret, and respond with intention instead of impulse. As life grows more complex, this quiet skill becomes one of our most powerful tools for navigating uncertainty. — Adama Coulibaly, *Positive Minds, The Wisdom Journal,* Issue 001.— https://adamacoulibaly.squarespace.com/the-wisdom-journal/the-power-of-perspective.

Gaining a spiritual perspective is not a cure for every uncertainty we may have regarding the Bible. Many people view the world through spiritual eyes, but the clarity of that vision can be clouded by tradition and false assumptions.

An example of someone with constricted spiritual vision is Saul of Tarsus. We are introduced to Saul in the seventh chapter of Acts during the stoning of Stephen.

> But he [Stephen], being full of the Holy Spirit, looked intently into heaven and saw the glory of God, and Jesus standing at the right hand of God. And he said, "Behold, I see the heavens opened and the Son of Man standing at the right hand of God!"
> But crying out with a loud voice, they stopped their ears and rushed at him with one purpose. And after they had driven him out of the city, they began to stone him, *and the witnesses laid aside their cloaks at the feet of a young man named Saul.* And they kept on stoning Stephen as he was calling out and saying, "Lord Jesus, receive my spirit!" And falling to his knees, he cried out with a loud voice, "Lord, do not hold this sin against them!" And after he said this, he fell asleep. *And Saul was agreeing with his murder.*
> Now there happened on that day a great persecution against the church in Jerusalem, and they were all scattered throughout the regions of Judea and Samaria, except the apostles. And devout men buried Stephen and made loud lamentation over him. *But Saul was attempting to destroy the church.* Entering house after house, he dragged off both men and women and delivered them to prison. — *Acts 7:55-60; 8:1-3 LEB,* (*emphasis mine*).

We return to Saul in chapter nine, when his perspective changes.

> *But Saul, still breathing threats and murder against the disciples of the Lord*, went to the high priest and asked for letters from him to the synagogues in Damascus, so that if he found any who were of the Way, both men and women, he could bring them tied up to Jerusalem.
> Now as he proceeded, it happened that when he approached Damascus, suddenly a light from heaven flashed around him. And falling to the ground, he heard a voice saying to him, "Saul, Saul, why are you persecuting me?"
> So he said, "Who are you, Lord?" And he said, "I am Jesus, whom you are persecuting! But get up and enter into the city, and it will be told to you what you must do."
> (Now the men who were traveling together with him stood speechless, because they heard the voice but saw no one.)
> So Saul got up from the ground, but although his eyes were open, he could see nothing. And leading him by the hand, they brought him into Damascus. — *Acts 9:1-8 LEB*, (*emphasis mine*).

Saul thought he was justified in his effort to persecute Christians, whom he deemed disloyal to the Law of Moses. It took a direct intervention by the resurrected Jesus to stop him.

Ananias was told by the Lord to find Saul, and he was stunned by the request.

> But Ananias replied, "Lord, I have heard from many people about this man, how much harm he has done

> to your saints in Jerusalem, and here he has authority from the chief priests to tie up all who call upon your name!"
> But the Lord said to him, "Go, because this man is my chosen instrument to carry my name before Gentiles and kings and the sons of Israel." — *Acts 9:13-15 LEB.*

Like his spiritual vision, Saul's physical vision was blinded by the event. The restoration of his sight by Ananias added weight to the reality that he had been misled by his religious tradition. The zeal he demonstrated for the Law was re-directed and he became an apostle to the nations, known as Paul (see Acts 13:9).

Paul's change in perspective had to be forced; that was the only way his course could be altered toward the Road to Life. Jesus knew Paul's zeal was perfect for his assignment and would propel him past all the obstacles that lay on the road before him.

Our perspective also needs adjusting. Perhaps not as drastically as Paul's, but course corrections are necessary for a successful Christian journey. Our personal reality must adopt the biblical worldview if we ever hope to walk the Road to Life.

Chapter 6

Symbolic Truth

> Our perspective is our reality; it is our truth filtered through our emotions, beliefs, culture, and life experiences. It shapes the way we interpret and make sense of reality, coloring our perceptions with shades of bias, prejudice, and preconceived notions. —Laura Bradshaw, *Truth vs. Perspective*, JourneyU, 2025. https://journeyu.org/blogs/truth-vs.-perspective

People can come to an agreement regarding truth. How? By using discernment to separate myth from reality. The truth of any matter can be found if we set aside emotion, cultural influences, and personal opinions. We must allow the data to create a path of evidence that will lead to an obvious conclusion, without bias getting in the way. This process will produce a result with a firm foundation of facts; an undeniable, unbreakable reality.

To achieve this reality takes effort. To comprehend the true biblical worldview as understood by those who wrote the scriptures, we must become a studious learner. The word in Greek is μαθητής (măthāytāys), which is most often translated in the NT as disciple, and has the basic meaning: a learner, one who seeks to learn from another.

> A disciple is not only a partaker of information but also one who seeks to become like his or her teacher (See Luke 6:40)— Chris Byrley, *Discipleship*, in *Lexham Theological Wordbook,* ed. Douglas Mangum et al., Lexham Bible Reference Series (Bellingham, WA: Lexham Press, 2014).

We need to adopt the understanding revealed in scripture. This may not be obvious because our perception must adjust to the perspectives of the authors. One of the most persistent characteristics of every prophet in the Bible is their habit of using hyperbole; extravagant exaggeration to emphasize importance.

A person today may use hyperbole in everyday conversations about sports: "The San Diego Chargers *annihilated* the Pittsburgh Steelers 37 to 7." The Chargers didn't actually *annihilate* (kill in large numbers) the Steelers, they just had more points when the game time ended. They won.

This type of exaggeration is common when we want to emphasize the outcome of something, either due to pride for the victors or a personal victory: "I *crushed* that exam!" Really? You may have achieved a high score, but you didn't "compress with violence" or "distort by pressure," the exam.

Metaphors, Idioms and other types of expressions may have implied meanings in the past that have been lost to modern cultures. In American English, the phrase "pay attention" may be difficult to comprehend by someone who was raised speaking a different language, who may say "give attention" in their native tongue. Although "give" is the original meaning of "pay" (*Oxford English Dictionary:* to render, bestow, or give), the modern association of the word "pay" with monetary compensation can result in a misapplied meaning for a foreign speaker.

When words are understood to be literal when they are intended to be non-literal, or when an ancient understanding is obscured by modern translators, the intent of the original author can get mired in misapplied meaning.

Metaphor in the Bible

> **God's Wrath and Eschatological Fire.** In what seems to us to be bold anthropomorphism, God's anger burns like a fire (Hos 8:5). It is hot, and he pours it out like fire (Nahum 1:6; cf. Lam 2:4). Isaiah 66:15 (God comes in fire to "render his anger in fury") and Jeremiah 15:14 (God says, "in my anger a fire is kindled which shall burn forever"; cf. 17:4) are typical. Prophecies of destruction by fire are often simply figurative ways of saying that God's judgment is sure or thorough. —Leland Ryken et al., *Dictionary of Biblical Imagery* (Downers Grove, IL: InterVarsity Press, 2000), page 288.

Fire as a metaphor has led to misconceptions when taken to be a literal outcome. The *Lake of Fire* in Revelation (19:20, 20:10,14,15) is an example of metaphor. We know this because of the context, but the context may not be obvious.

> And the beast was seized, and with him the false prophet who performed the signs before him, by which he deceived those who received the mark of the beast and those who had worshiped his image. The two were thrown alive into the lake of fire that burns with sulfur. — *Revelation 19:20 LEB.*

> And the devil who deceived them was thrown into the lake of fire and sulphur, where the beast and the false prophet also are, and they will be tormented day and night forever and ever. — *Revelation 20:10 LEB.*

The word "tormented" in the *Lexham English Bible* is the common English translation of the Greek word, βασανίζω (bǎsǎnid´zō). "Tormented" is used because the translators are taking the "Lake of Fire" as a literal place where the wicked will suffer eternally, "day and night forever and ever" This ignores the metaphorical use of fire as a destructive force that imparts a moment of "torment" to those thrown into it, but who are then annihilated from existence. A better English translation is the word "punishment," which is used in the *Bible in Basic English,* because whatever is thrown into the Lake of Fire is punished with "destruction." The fire destroys them. A punishment that can never be reversed, so it lasts forever.

> The beast that you saw was, and is not, and is about to rise from the bottomless pit and go to destruction. —*Revelation 17:8 LEB.*

> But the wrongdoers will come to *destruction*, and the haters of the Lord will be like the fat of lambs, they will be burned up; they will go up in smoke, and never again be seen. — *Psalm 37:29 BBE.*

This agrees with the fate of the weeds in Jesus' parable.

> Gather the weeds first and bind them in bundles to be burned . . . Just as the weeds are gathered and burned with fire, so will it be at the end of the age. The Son

> of Man will send his angels, and they will gather out of his kingdom all causes of sin and all law-breakers, and throw them into the fiery furnace. In that place there will be weeping and gnashing of teeth. —*Matthew 13:30,40-42 ESV.*

βασανίζω (bǎsǎnid´zō) is a derivative of the root word βασανος (bǎsǎnŏs), which originally referred to a touchstone, a dark stone used to test the purity of gold and silver. Over time the meaning evolved to denote the means by which someone or something is tested or judged; "through the notion of going to the bottom," (see *The New Strong's Dictionary of Hebrew and Greek Words*. Nashville: Thomas Nelson, 1996), which implies thorough examination and was used to describe torture in some instances, but not all. βασανος (bǎsǎnŏs) is used in Matthew 18:34 to describe punishment by *jailers*.

> And in anger his master delivered him to the *jailers* (bǎsǎnŏs), until he should pay all his debt. —*Matthew 18:34 ESV.*

The purpose is *punishment*, not *torture*. We know this because Yahweh is not evil, and torture is evil.

> No one who is being tempted should say, "I am being tempted by God," for God cannot be tempted by evil, and he himself tempts no one. —*James 1:13 LEB.*

So the implication is that βασανίζω (bǎsǎnid´zō) is a judgment that will imprison the guilty in eternal "destruction." This becomes obvious when we understand the biblical effects of the "Lake of Fire."

> And Death and Hades were thrown into the Lake of Fire. This is the second death—the lake of fire. And if anyone was not found written in the book of life, he was thrown into the lake of fire. — *Revelation 20:14,15 LEB.*

So the metaphorical *Lake of Fire* is a symbol for the *Second Death*. The *Second Death* is a death with no possible resurrection, or complete annihilation, as stated in the following scripture:

> And if anyone was not found written in the Book of Life, he was thrown into the lake of fire . . . and death will not exist any longer, and mourning or wailing or pain will not exist any longer. The former things have passed away. — *Revelation 20:15; 21:4 LEB.*

The former things will not exist any longer: death, (which is thrown into the lake of fire), pain, wailing, mourning, and anyone not written in the Book of Life. All these things will be burned up (completely destroyed); a punishment that will last forever. If mourning, pain, and wailing "pass away" in the "Lake of Fire," there can be no eternal torment.

Only a conscious, living person can experience things. Those not in the Book of Life will lose their life; they will cease to experience anything forever. They will be annihilated.

> For to him who is joined with all the living there is hope; for a living dog is better than a dead lion. For the living know that they will die, but the dead don't know anything, neither do they have any more a

> reward; for their memory is forgotten. — *Ecclesiastes 9:4,5 WEB.*

This understanding also agrees with the punishment told to Adam:

> By the sweat of your face will you eat bread until you return to the ground, for out of it you were taken. For you are dust, and to dust you shall return. — *Genesis 3:19 WEB.*

Adam was not punished with torment; he was punished with death; a permanent loss of life.

> For the wages of sin is death, but the free gift of God is eternal life in Christ Jesus our Lord. — *Romans 6:23 WEB.*

> The soul who sins shall die. — *Ezekial 18:4 ESV.*

> And it will be that every soul who does not listen to that prophet will be destroyed utterly from the people. — *Acts 3:23 LEB.*

This is in harmony with other scriptural statements of what happens to the wicked.

> For behold, your enemies, O Yahweh, for behold, your enemies will *perish.* All the workers of evil will be scattered. — *Psalm 92:9 LEB.*

> Whenever they say "Peace and security," then sudden destruction will overtake them like the birth pains of a pregnant woman, and they will not possibly escape. — *1 Thessalonians 5:3 LEB.*

Burning as a symbol for punishment that lasts forever is also found in the prophecy about the punishment against the nation of Edom.

> The rivers of Edom will turn into tar, and the soil will turn into sulfur. The whole country will burn like tar. It will burn day and night, and smoke will rise from it forever. The land will lie waste age after age, and no one will ever travel through it again. — *Isaiah 34:9, 10 GNB.*

We know from observation that the smoke is not rising today and the country is not burning day and night. We know from the very next verse that owls and ravens will take over the land, indicating it will still be inhabited (Isaiah 34:11). The intent of this prophecy is revealed in verse 12:

> There will be no king to rule the country, and the leaders will all be gone. — *Isaiah 34:12 GNB.*

The nation of Edom was completely destroyed. There are no Edomites living today. The nation was metaphorically burned up.

> If Edom says. "We are shattered, but we will return and rebuild the ruins," Yahweh of hosts says this: "They may build, but I will tear down; and they will

> be called a territory of wickedness, and the people with whom Yahweh is angry forever" — *Malachi 1:4 LEB*

Allegory in the Bible

Allegory is another type of expression used throughout scripture. These are representations of abstract or spiritual ideas expressed using concrete or material items, or historical figures; an explanation of one subject using the guise of another.

> **The Garden of God.** Associated as it is with life at its fullest, one should not be surprised to find that the garden is one of the framing images of the total Bible story. In Genesis 2 Adam is provided the Garden of Eden as a perfect abode and workplace . . . If the Garden of Eden is an image of divine provision, it is paradoxically also a place of human labor. Gardens, after all, require cultivation. Genesis 2 tells us that God took the newly created Adam and "put him in the garden of Eden to till it and keep it" (Gen 2:15 NRSV) . . . The garden is a place prepared for humankind, but also a place requiring ongoing human upkeep . . . So are introduced two pervasive themes of the biblical record: God is ever providing a place as well as promising new and more perfect places, even as humankind is enjoined to collaborate in obedience to the unfolding divine purpose. —Leland Ryken et al., *Dictionary of Biblical Imagery* (Downers Grove, IL: InterVarsity Press, 2000), pages 315–316.

The divine purpose will be successful, despite Adam's rejection of Yahweh's authority and Satan's continuing efforts to uproot mankind's place in the divine purpose. No living creature can thwart Yahweh's plans. Their shortsighted understanding will end, and the Garden will fill the entire Earth.

> And the one seated on the throne said, "Behold, I am making all things new!" And he said, "Write, because these words are faithful and true"
> And he said to me, "It is done! I am the Alpha and the Omega, the beginning and the end. To the one who is thirsty I will give water from the spring of the water of life freely. The one who conquers will inherit these things, and I will be his God and he will be my son. But as for the cowards and unbelievers and detestable persons and murderers and sexually immoral people and sorcerers and idolaters and all liars, their share is in the lake that burns with fire and sulfur, which is the second death." — *Revelation 21:5-8 LEB.*

> For Yahweh will comfort Zion; he will comfort all its sites of ruins. And he will make its wilderness like Eden, and its desert like the garden of Yahweh. Joy and gladness will be found in it, thanksgiving and the sound of song. — *Isaiah 51:3 LEB.*

In his letter to the Galatians, Paul used Sarah and Hagar as an allegory for a greater spiritual understanding, leading to his quotation of Isaiah 54:1.

Tell me, you who are wanting to be under the law, do you not understand the law? For it is written that Abraham had two sons, one by the female slave and one by the free woman. But the one by the female slave was born according to human descent, and the one by the free woman through the promise, which things are spoken allegorically, for these women are two covenants, one from Mount Sinai, bearing children for slavery, who is Hagar. Now Hagar is Mount Sinai in Arabia, and corresponds to the present Jerusalem, for she is a slave with her children. But the Jerusalem above is free, which is our mother. For it is written:
"Rejoice, O barren woman, who does not give birth to children; burst out and shout, you who do not have birth pains, because many are the children of the desolate woman, even more than those of the one who has a husband." — *Galatians: 4: 21-27 LEB.*

In this allegory of Sarah and Hagar, it is important to notice that Paul is not dealing with the principle of evil within our hearts, but with the attempt to mingle two dispensations or methods of religious experience—the Law and the Gospel. —*Through the Bible Day by Day*, F.B. Meyer, Galatians 4:21-31, 1914.

In order to show fully the nature and the effect of the Law, Paul here introduces an illustration from an important fact in Jewish history . . . He uses it simply, as showing the difference between servitude

> and freedom, and as a striking illustration of the nature of the bondage to the Jewish law, and of the freedom of the gospel, just as anyone may use a striking historical fact to illustrate a principle. — Albert Barnes, *Notes on the Bible,* Galatians 4:21, Published in 1847-1885.

Metaphor and allegory are two types of expressions that build pictures to help us understand God's word, if we perceive the intent behind their use and avoid taking what they imply literally.

Chapter 7

Not the Word of God

The Mosaic Law was given to help the children of Abraham draw closer to Yahweh and benefit from a deep relationship with the Creator. It was meant to protect them from a lawless world until the Messiah arrived.

> Why then the law? It was added because of transgressions until the offspring should come to whom the promise had been made . . . So then, the law was our guardian until Christ came, in order that we might be justified by faith. — *Galatians 3:19,24 ISV.*

The Greek word translated "guardian" in the *International Standard Version is* παιδαγωγός (paidagōgŏs):

> A servant whose office it was to take the children to school; (by implication [figuratively] a *tutor* ["*pædagogue*"]):— instructor, schoolmaster. —*The New Strong's Dictionary of Hebrew and Greek Words.* Nashville: Thomas Nelson, 1996.

A *pedagogue* in ancient Greece was more than a tutor or instructor. A pedagogue was also a protector; a servant who had the responsibility to escort and protect the child to and from school. Therefore, the translation to "guardian" in the *ISV*.

A modern equivalent to the ancient pedagogue would be a school bus driver who also instructs the children. The purpose of the Mosaic Law was mandated until the arrival of the Messiah. Why then, once the Messiah came, did the majority of the Jews not get off the bus? They stayed on the bus (under the mandates of the Law) because they failed to recognize that the Messiah had come. This lack of spiritual insight was due to the centuries of traditions added to the Law. They were so entangled in their own perspectives they failed to understand the spirit of the Law and demanded adherence to the expanded tradition of rules and regulations that had been added to the Law. The additions created a "fence" around God's written Law to ensure people would not break it, but this evolved into burdensome, man-made rules prioritizing ritual over the spiritual aspect of the Law.

> It cannot be denied that the religion of Israel passed through many changes. It grew and purified and spiritualized itself out of its own inherent strength; but it also suffered many relapses, when hindering and corrupting influence gained the upper hand. —James Orr, Editor, 1929, *International Standard Bible Encyclopedia*, 1980 Edition, Eerdmans Publishing Company, Vol.3, Page 1541.

The corrupting influence within Judaism was revealed by the Messiah in his comments to the scribes and Pharisees in Matthew, chapter 23. Messiah's declarations of woe revealed the hypocrisy of the religious leaders and the judgment they would receive, while prompting them to focus on the spiritual aspects of the Law that impact the heart. (See Matthew 23:1-36).

> Here we have [Christ's] discourse concerning them, or rather against them. I. He allows their office (Mat 23:2, Mat 23:3). II. He warns his disciples not to imitate their hypocrisy and pride (Mat 23: 4-12). III. He exhibits a charge against them for diverse high crimes and misdemeanors, corrupting the law, opposing the gospel, and treacherous dealing both with God and man; and to each article he prefixes a woe . . . Now each of these woes against the scribes and Pharisees has a reason annexed to it, containing a separate crime charged upon them, proving their hypocrisy and justifying the judgment of Christ upon them. —*Matthew Henry's Commentary on the Whole Bible, Matthew 23*, 1708-1714, Public Domain.

The Gospel of Mark focuses on other aspects of the man-made tradition added to the Law.

> Then the Pharisees and some of the scribes gathered together to him, having come from Jerusalem. Now when they saw some of his disciples eating bread with defiled, that is unwashed, hands, they found fault. (For the Pharisees and all the Jews, don't eat unless they wash their hands and forearms, holding to the tradition of the elders. They don't eat when they come from the marketplace unless they bathe themselves, and there are many other things, which

> they have received to hold to: washings of cups, pitchers, bronze vessels, and couches.)
> The Pharisees and the scribes asked him, "Why don't your disciples walk according to the tradition of the elders, but eat their bread with unwashed hands?"
> He answered them, "Well did Isaiah prophesy of you hypocrites, as it is written, 'This people honors me with their lips, but their heart is far from me. But they worship me in vain, teaching as doctrines the commandments of men.' "For you set aside the commandment of God, and hold tightly to the tradition of men—the washing of pitchers and cups, and you do many other such things."
> He said to them, "Full well do you reject the commandment of God, that you may keep your tradition." — *Mark 7:1-9 WEB.*

Tradition is not the Word of God. It may encompass the Word of God, but it adds to it in a way that corrupts the original intent. It changes heart-felt devotion to legalistic adherence to man-made mandates.

Paul warned against adding things to God's Word in his second letter to Timothy.

> For the time is coming when people will not endure sound teaching, but having itching ears they will accumulate for themselves teachers to suit their own passions, and will turn away from listening to the truth and wander off into myths. — *2 Timothy 4:3,4 ESV.*

The Amplified Bible (1987 Edition), says it this way:

> For the time is coming when [*people*] will not tolerate (endure) sound *and* wholesome instruction, but, having ears itching *[for something pleasing and gratifying]*, they will gather to themselves one teacher after another to a considerable number, chosen to satisfy their own liking *and* to foster the errors they hold, And will turn aside from hearing the truth and wander off into myths *and* man-made fictions. — *2 Timothy 4:3,4 AMP.*

This attitude has been persistent since the 1st-century among those who profess to be Christians.

> But even in the apostolic age many Jews and Gentiles were baptized only with water, not the Holy Spirit and fire of the gospel, and smuggled their old religious notions and practices into the church. Hence the heretical tendencies, which are combated in the New Testament, especially in the Pauline and Catholic Epistles. — Philip Schaff, 1890, *History of the Christian Church*, 5th edition, *The Complete Eight Volumes in One*, page 928.

Philip Schaff's assessment is proven true by statements in the following scriptures:

> Just as I urged you when I traveled to Macedonia, remain in Ephesus, so that you may instruct certain people not to teach other doctrine, and not to pay

attention to myths and endless genealogies, which cause useless speculations rather than God's plan that is by faith. But the goal of our instruction is love from a pure heart and a good conscience and a faith without hypocrisy, from which some have deviated, and have turned away into fruitless discussion, wanting to be teachers of the law, although they do not understand either the things which they are saying or the things concerning which they are speaking confidently. — *1 Timothy 1:3-7 LEB*

Make every effort to present yourself approved to God, a worker having no need to be ashamed, guiding the word of truth along a straight path. But avoid pointless chatter, for it will progress to greater ungodliness, and their message will spread like gangrene, among whom are Hymenaeus and Philetus, who have deviated concerning the truth by saying the resurrection has already taken place, and they are upsetting the faith of some. However, the solid foundation of God stands firm, having this seal: "The Lord knows those who are his," and "Everyone who names the name of the Lord must abstain from unrighteousness" — *2 Timothy 2:15-19 LEB*

And regard the patience of our Lord as salvation, just as also our dear brother Paul wrote to you, according to the wisdom that was given to him, as he does also in all his letters, speaking in them about these things, in which there are some things hard to understand,

> which the ignorant and unstable distort to their own destruction, as they also do the rest of the scriptures. — *2 Peter 3:15,16 LEB*

> For there are many rebellious people, idle talkers and deceivers, especially those with Jewish connections, who must be silenced because they mislead whole families by teaching for dishonest gain what ought not to be taught. A certain one of them, in fact, one of their own prophets, said, "Cretans are always liars, evil beasts, lazy gluttons" Such testimony is true. For this reason rebuke them sharply that they may be healthy in the faith, and not pay attention to Jewish myths and commands of people who reject the truth. All is pure to those who are pure. But to those who are corrupt and unbelieving, nothing is pure, but both their minds and consciences are corrupted. They profess to know God, but with their deeds they deny him, since they are detestable, disobedient, and unfit for any good deed. — *Titus 1:10-16 NET*

Paul wrote to the churches in Galatia because some were following "a different gospel." (Galatians 1:6). He says, "There are certain people who are troubling you and want to distort the gospel about the Messiah." (Galatians 1:7). He then stresses the importance of what he is about to say:

> But even if we or an angel from heaven should proclaim to you a gospel contrary to what we proclaimed to you, let that person be condemned! What we have told you in the past, I am

> now telling you again: If anyone proclaims to you a gospel contrary to what you received, let that person be condemned! Am I now trying to win the approval of people or of God? Or am I trying to please people? If I were still trying to please people, I would not be the Messiah's servant. — *Galatians 1:8-10 LEB.*

Paul later reminds those Jews in the churches that the Law has been made mute by the sacrifice Jesus made on the cross, and that turning back to the Law will nullify what Jesus accomplished.

> We ourselves are Jews by birth, and not gentile sinners, yet we know that a person is not justified by doing what the Law requires, but rather by the faithfulness of Jesus the Messiah. We too have believed in the Messiah Jesus so that we might be justified by the faithfulness of the Messiah and not by doing what the Law requires, for no human being will be justified by doing what the Law requires . . . I do not misapply God's grace, for if righteousness comes about by doing what the Law requires, then the Messiah died for nothing. — *Galatians 2:15,16[1],21 ISV.*

Paul then turns his attention to the gentile Galatians who turned to serve God by accepting the Messiah's sacrifice.

> But now, because you have come to know God, or rather have come to be known by God, how can you turn back again to the weak and miserable elemental spirits? Do you want to be enslaved to them all over

> again? You carefully observe days and months and seasons and years. I am afraid for you, lest perhaps I have labored for you in vain! — *Galatians 4:9-11 LEB.*

These two points are important for us to remember:

> **1.** The Jews were no longer obligated to observe what Yahweh had once commanded them to observe (which includes all festivals, feasts, and sacrifices) because the Law was nullified by Christ's death and resurrection.
>
> **2.** Gentile converts to Christianity were no longer expected to observe festivals, feasts, and sacrifices to their pagan gods. Their ceremonial observances (days and months and seasons and years), which Yahweh had never commanded them to observe, were now null and void for pure worship through Jesus the Messiah. Traditional yearly observances that had their origin in pagan religion are of no value. By incorporating them into Christian worship, they invalidate our relationship with God.

Just as the Mosaic Law was corrupted by religious sects who added man-made rules to the Law, 1st-century Christianity has been corrupted by various sects adding ideas and rules to the way of faith proclaimed by Jesus and the Apostles. This has led to the multi-denominational *Christendom* of the 21st-century. The various denominations diverge in many areas and demonstrate how far faith can travel down roads that lead away from the Word of God, back into pagan concepts that twist scripture.

In Leo Rosten's book, *Religions of America,* he presents answers to questions he sent to "the sixteen largest denominations in the United States" (*Religions of America*, 1975 edition, page 17). After reading all the answers to Rosten's questions, and then reviewing all the data collected in the 321 page Almanac that follows, it becomes obvious how much the Christian faith has moved away from the Word of God, and wrapped Christiandom in a bundle of religious concepts that originated from pagan sources.

Understanding the current state of Christendom, we must contemplate the following scripture with the same focus as a 1st-century disciple in Galatia.

> For freedom Christ has set us free. Stand firm, therefore, and do not be subject again to a yoke of slavery. — *Galatians 5:1 LEB.*

Chapter Notes

1. Galatians 2:16

Paul's explanation about the difference between works of the Law and faith has been translated two different ways.

> **1.** Some translations (ASV, LEB, ESV, GNB, etc.) put the act of faith upon the believer, which brings salvation.
>
> **2.** Other translations (ISV, NET, KJV, DRB, etc.) put the act of faith upon the Messiah, which brings salvation to believers.

Following Paul's argument that human actions (works of the Law) cannot bring salvation, along with the grammatical fact that the reference to the Messiah in the verse is in the genitive case (κριστοῦ, christou: of Christ), the second option fits the context better.

Without Jesus demonstrating unfailing faith in Yahweh, his Father, ("Not my will, but your will," Mark 14:36; Luke 22:42), our salvation would not be possible. Our salvation cannot be gained by works, but is a free gift based on our belief in the faithfulness of the Messiah.

Part Three

The Life

Life is a gift. It is not something we are owed. We cannot buy it or steal it, but we can lose it.

CHAPTER 8

FAITHFULNESS OF THE MESSIAH

How are we justified by the faithfulness of the Messiah?

People who lived in the past, and everyone who will ever live in our lawless world, have always, and will always, die because of one man. That man was Adam, and his legacy is lawlessness and death.

Jesus the Messiah is the way. In other words, he is the fulfillment of God's means to redeem Adam's offspring from a life that only leads to death. All other options are false; the hope they claim to hold will always fail and end in death. So we are freed from a hopeless future and the shackles of useless ideology that will never end in eternal life.

But how is it possible for one man to be the only hope for an eternal future for billions of people?

Paul explains it this way:

> For since through a man came death, also through a man came the resurrection of the dead. For just as in Adam all die, so also in Christ all will be made alive. . . . Thus also it is written, "The first man, Adam, became a living soul"; the last Adam became a life-giving spirit. — *1 Corinthians 15:21,22,45 LEB.*

The identity of the Messiah as the "Last Adam" is not talked about enough, and because of that, has not been a prominent reality in the minds of most modern-day Christians. The context of the verses quoted from 1 Corinthians is Paul's discussion about the resurrection being the solution for the death caused by Adam. Earlier in the letter, Paul says this:

> For you were bought at a price. — *1 Corinthians 6:20 LEB*

What was that price?

The Messiah's life was the price. Jesus was born a sinless human being; not from the line of Adam, because he had existed as an Elohim, a heavenly being, and was transferred into Mary's womb by Yahweh. This act fulfilled the first prophecy in Genesis as he is the "seed [offspring] of the woman" (see Genesis 3:15). He was the equal to Adam, a sinless creation, which is why Paul calls him "the last Adam."

Adam and Eve were made perfect with the ability to live forever, provided they lived in harmony with their creator's will. Once they rejected Yahweh's sovereignty, they were removed from the garden and eventually died. While they remained alive, Adam and Eve had children. While Adam and Eve willfully sinned, their children did not, but would still face the same end because they can only inherit what their parents passed on to them; a life separated from their Creator, because they were born from the union of sinful parents and into a lawless world.

Amid this rebellion, Yahweh's will for the Earth must still be fulfilled. He had charged Adam to multiply and fill the Earth (Genesis 1:28), which is why he allowed Adam and Eve to not suffer immediate death, but to produce offspring to fulfill God's expressed word.

> For just as the rain and the snow come down from heaven, and they do not return there except they have watered the earth thoroughly and cause it to bring forth and sprout, and give seed to the sower and bread to the eater, so shall be my word that goes out from my mouth. It shall not return to me without success, but shall accomplish what I desire and be successful in the thing for which I sent it. — *Isaiah 55:10,11 LEB.*

Because Adam and Eve's offspring did not choose to be born into a lawless world, their suffering the same fate as their parents is not in harmony with Yahweh's justice. To redeem them from death due to Adam's sin, a reconciliation between Yahweh and Adam's offspring had to be made.

The reconciliation, to be of value, had to be due to more than just a physical equal to Adam. It had to be spiritually superior to Adam; a sinless example of perfect integrity to Yahweh. This accomplished two things:

> **1.** It proved a sinless creation is capable of maintaining integrity to Yahweh's will under any circumstance, even the terrible scourging and painful death of crucifixion.
>
> **2.** By maintaining his loyalty to Yahweh, Jesus retained the value of his life, which he could have passed on to his children through genetic inheritance. The possibility of producing his own progeny is what

Jesus willingly exchanged for the salvation of Adam's sinful offspring; he adopted them instead of producing his own. Therefore, the following statements by Paul:

> For you have not received a spirit of slavery leading to fear again, but you have received the Spirit of adoption, by whom we cry out, "Abba! Father!" — *Romans 8:15 LEB.*

> Not only this, but we ourselves also, having the first fruits of the Spirit, even we ourselves groan within ourselves while we await eagerly our adoption, the redemption of our body. — *Romans 8:23 LEB.*

> But when the fullness of time came, God sent out his Son, born of a woman, born under the law, in order that he might redeem those under the law, in order that we might receive the adoption. — *Galatians 4:4,5 LEB.*

> Blessed is the God and Father of our Lord Jesus Christ, who has blessed us with every spiritual blessing in the heavenly places in Christ . . . having predestined us to adoption through Jesus Christ to himself according to the good pleasure of his will. — *Ephesians 1:3,5 LEB.*

This adoption is only possible because of the love of Yahweh for Adam's lawless offspring, and because of the integrity of Jesus.

> For in this way God loved the world, so that he gave his one and only Son, in order that everyone who believes in him will not perish, but will have eternal life. — *John 3:16 LEB.*

> For there is one God and one mediator between God and human beings, the man Christ Jesus, who gave himself a ransom for all. — 1 Timothy 2:5,6 LEB.

The Only Begotten Son

Before moving forward, it is important to note that the term "his one and only Son" in the *Lexham English Bible* (John 3:16) is a modern translation of the original Greek. Other English translations have "only begotten son" (AMP, KJV, DRB, ASV, LSV), which is more faithful to the Greek original.

> Γὰρ [For] Οὕτως [in this way] ὁ [the] θεὸς [God] ἠγάπησεν [love] τὸν [the] κόσμον [world] ὥστε [so] ἔδωκεν [that he gave], τὸν [his] τὸν [the] μονογενῆ [only begotten] υἱὸν [son]. — *John 3:16a TGNT.*

> Μονογενῆ, (mŏnŏgĕnay) is the adjective, accusative, singular, masculine form of the root, μονογενής, (mŏnŏgĕnays); only born, i.e. sole: — only (begotten, child). — *The New Strong's Dictionary of Hebrew and Greek Words.* Nashville: Thomas Nelson, 1996.

However, based on other scriptures, Yahweh has many sons:

Then the **sons of God** saw the daughters of humankind. — *Genesis 6:2 LEB.*

When the Most High gave to the nations their inheritance, when he divided mankind, he fixed the borders of the peoples according to the number of the **sons of God**. — *Deuteronomy 32:8*[1] *ESV.*

And it happened one day that the **sons of God** came to present themselves before Yahweh, and Satan also came into their midst. — *Job 1:6 LEB.*

And then one day the **sons of God** came to present themselves before Yahweh, and Satan also came into their midst to present himself before Yahweh. — *Job 2:1 LEB.*

Where were you at my laying the foundation of the earth? Tell me if you possess understanding. Who determined its measurement? . . . On what were its bases sunk? Or who laid its cornerstone, when the morning stars were singing together and all the **sons of God** shouted for joy? — Job 38:4 LEB.

Blessed are the peacemakers, because they will be called **sons of God**. — *Matthew 5:9 LEB.*

For they are not even able to die any longer, because they are like the angels and are **sons of God**, because they are sons of the resurrection. — *Luke 20:36 LEB.*

> For all those who are led by the Spirit of God, these are **sons of God**. — *Romans 8:14 LEB.*

> And it will be in the place where it was said to them, "You are not my people," there they will be called "**sons of the living God.**" — *Romans 9:26 LEB.*

> For you are all **sons of God** through faith in Christ Jesus. — *Galatians 3:26 LEB.*

So what is the significance of calling Jesus "the Only Begotten Son?"

Mŏnŏgĕnays is a combination of two Greek words, Μονος, mŏnŏs (only, alone, one) and γινομαι, ginŏmai (be, become). Ginŏmai implies a being with a beginning. Jesus is the only son directly produced (created) by Yahweh, his one and only son, because he was "begotten," or "came to be."

At John 6:57 Jesus says, "I live because of the Father." Only Yahweh has life in himself. His name means "the self-existing one," who is the source of all creation (Psalm 148:1-5), and has no beginning.

> Before the mountains were born and you brought forth the earth and the world, even from everlasting to everlasting, you are God. — *Psalm 90:2 LEB.*

> Yahweh is king; he clothes himself with majesty. Yahweh clothes himself; he girds himself with might. Yes, the world is established so that it will not be moved. Your throne is established from of old; you are from everlasting. — *Psalm 93:1,2 LEB.*

> But Yahweh is the true God, he is the living God and an everlasting king. —*Jeremiah 10:10 LEB.*

All created beings owe their existence, their life, to Yahweh. Revelation 3:14 says about Jesus, "And to the angel of the church in Laodicea write: The words of the Amen, the faithful and true witness, the beginning[2] of God's creation," which agrees with Colossians 1:15 ("the firstborn of all creation"), and Proverbs 8:22-30, where wisdom refers to the Messiah[3] ("The first of his [Yahweh's] ways," who "was brought forth,"[4] and was "beside him [Yahweh] as a master workman.") Compare Psalm 2:7[5] and Hebrews 1:5. All other heavenly sons were produced through Jesus. This explains Paul's statement at 1 Corinthians 8:6:

> Yet to us there is one God, the Father, from whom are all things, and we are for him, and there is one Lord, Jesus Christ, through whom are all things, and we are through him. — *1 Corinthians 8:6 LEB.*

Understanding the uniqueness of the Only Begotten Son, and his relationship with the other heavenly "Sons of God," helps us understand the position he was in before Yahweh transferred him into Mary's womb. Paul explains:

> Have this in your mind, which was also in Christ Jesus, who, existing in the form of God, didn't consider equality with God a thing to be grasped, but emptied himself, taking the form of a servant, being made in the likeness of men. And being found in human form, he humbled himself, becoming

> obedient to the point of death, yes, the death of the cross. — *Philippians 2:5-8 WEB.*

The two uses of the word "God" in Philippians 2:6 (θεοῦ, thĕou: the genitive, singular, masculine form of θεός, thĕŏs, and θεῷ, thĕō: the dative, singular, masculine form of θεός, thĕŏs), are both indefinite nouns in the sentence, because there is no definite article (the) that proceeds them.

> ὃς [who] ὑπάρχων [existing] ἐν [in] μορφῇ [form] θεοῦ [of a god] οὐχ [did not] ἡγήσατο [consider] τὸ [the] εἶναι [being] ἴσα [equal] θεῷ [to a god] ἁρπαγμὸν [something to be grasped]. — *Philippians 2: 6 TGNT.*

If the definite article was used with the nouns (τοὺ θεοῦ, tou thĕou, "of the God," and τῷ θεῷ, tō thĕō, "to the god," they would be a direct reference to Yahweh, the one and only Almighty God. Since the references are indefinite, the phrases refer to "form of a god" and "equal to a god," both of which identify a generic heavenly being. Since all heavenly beings are called in Hebrew, eloah, (god), or elohim, (gods), the Greek, θεός (god), is often used similarly in the NT (see John 1:1, Acts 28:6).

At Hebrews 2:7 the Hebrew "elohim" was translated from Psalm 8 to the Greek, ἀγγέλους (angĕlous), the neuter, plural, masculine form of the root, αγγελος (angĕlŏs); messenger; angel, which verifies the use of "elohim" for all heavenly beings. (Compare Psalm 8:4,5; Hebrews 2:6,7).

> **Than the angels** — Hebrew, "than God," "Elohim," that is, the abstract qualities of God, such as angels possess in an inferior form; namely, heavenly,

> spiritual, incorporeal natures. — *Commentary Critical and Explanatory on the Whole Bible*, Jamieson, Fausset, and Brown, vol. 2 (Oak Harbor, WA: Logos Research Systems, Inc., 1997), page 444.

Paul is writing in his letter to the Philippians about the attitude Jesus had before becoming human. Jesus was in the "form" of a god, μορφῇ, morphē̆: shape; figuratively nature: form (*The New Strong's Dictionary of Hebrew and Greek Word*s. Nashville: Thomas Nelson, 1996), which fits the OT understanding that all who dwell in the spirit realm are elohim; they all have spirit bodies. Although having a spirit body in his pre-human existence, Jesus did not try to retain that form of existence. He did not "grasp" at equality with heavenly beings. The Greek word translated "grasp" in the text is ἁρπαγμὸν, harpăgmŏn: the accusative, singular, masculine form of the root ἁρπάζω, harpădzō, which means: to seize (in various applications): catch (away, up), pluck, pull, take-by force, (*The New Strong's Dictionary of Hebrew and Greek Words*. Nashville: Thomas Nelson, 1996).

To be able to sacrifice his life for Adam's offspring, Jesus had to die. Only a created being can die. Because Yahweh is immortal and thus incorruptible, He cannot degrade to a lower state of existence; Yahweh cannot die. (Job 36:26; 1 Timothy 1:17).

Jesus died, and because of his faithfulness, he was exalted to a superior position.

> Therefore also God [Yahweh] exalted him [Jesus] and graciously granted him the name above every name, so that at the name of Jesus every knee should bow, of those in heaven and of those on earth and of those under the earth, and every tongue confess that

> Jesus Christ is Lord, to the glory of God [Yahweh] the Father. — *Philippians 2:9-11 LEB.*

This agrees with Paul's discussion in his letter to the Colossians:

> He [Jesus] is the image of the invisible God [Yahweh], the firstborn of all creation. For by him all things were created, in heaven and on earth, visible and invisible, whether thrones or dominions or rulers or authorities—all things were created through him and for him. And he is before all things, and in him all things hold together. And he is the head of the body, the church. He is the beginning, the firstborn from the dead, that in everything he might be preeminent. — *Colossians 1:15-18 ESV.*

These statements by Paul are expressions of the status of lineage; the first in a long line, not the originator of the lineage. Yahweh is the originator, the Father of all creation. Jesus was the first part of that creation, the firstborn. And because of that, Yahweh made a way for his only begotten son to be preeminent; first in all things created and the first human to be resurrected as a spirit being; the rightful heir of all things.

> Although God spoke long ago in many parts and in many ways to the fathers by the prophets, in these last days he has spoken to us by a Son, whom he appointed heir of all things, through whom also he made the world. — *Hebrews 1:1,2 LEB.*

The faithfulness of the Messiah elevated him to a superior position in heaven as the faithful savior sent by Yahweh to die for Adam's lawless offspring.

> Grace to you and peace from God the Father, and our Lord Jesus Christ, who gave himself for our sins, that he might deliver us out of this present evil age, according to the will of our God and Father— to whom be the glory forever and ever. Amen. —*Galatians 1:3-5 WEB.*

Chapter Notes

1. Based on the Septuagint and the Dead Sea Scroll 4Q37.

2. ἀρχὴ archay. The word properly refers to the "commencement" of a thing, not its "authorship," and denotes properly primacy in time, and primacy in rank, but not primacy in the sense of causing anything to exist. —Albert Barnes, *Notes on the Bible, Revelation 3:14*, Published in 1847-1885.

3. "Wisdom here is Christ" —Matthew Henry's *Commentary on the Whole Bible,* Proverbs 8:12-21, Published in 1708-1714; public domain.

The entire discussion about Wisdom in Proverbs 8:12-30 is seen by many as a representation of the pre-human Jesus, who was "brought forth" and assisted Yahweh as a "master workman" during the creation of the heavens, the earth and all life therein. This parallels John 1:3 and Colossians 1:16–17, which identifies Jesus as the Only Begotten Son through whom Yahweh created everything else in the physical universe and the spiritual realm.

4. **Was brought fourth (**Proverbs 8:24): The following scriptures demonstrate how different translations present the personified Wisdom as a created being.

Proverbs 8: 22,24

The LORD **made me as the beginning** of His way, the first of His works of old. . . . When there were no depths, I was **brought forth.** JPS.

Yahweh **possessed me at the beginning** of His way, Before His deeds of old . . . When there were no depths I was **brought forth** (or **Born**). LSB.

Yahweh **created me, the first of his ways,** before his acts of old . . . When there were no depths, I **was brought forth**. LEB.

The LORD **created me first of all**, the first of his works, long ago . . . **I was born** before the oceans, when there were no springs of water. GNB.

The LORD **created me as the beginning of his works**, before his deeds of long ago . . . When there were no deep oceans **I was born**, when there were no springs overflowing with water. NET.

Yahweh **possessed me in the beginning** of his work, before his deeds of old . . . When there were no depths, **I was born,** when there were no springs abounding with water. WEB.

The LORD **created and possessed me at the beginning of His way**, Before His works of old [were accomplished] . . . When there were no ocean depths **I was born**, When there were no fountains and springs overflowing with water. AMP - 2015.

The Lord **formed and brought me [Wisdom] forth at the beginning** of His way, before His acts of old . . . When there were no deeps, **I was brought forth**, when there were no fountains laden with water. AMP - 1987.

The Lord **made me as the start of his way,** the first of his works in the past . . . When there was no deep **I was given birth**, when there were no fountains flowing with water. BBE.

From the beginning, I was with the LORD. I was there before he began to create the earth . . . **When I was born**, there were no oceans or springs of water. CEV.

[5]**Begotten** (Psalm 2:7): yâlad, yaw-lad'; a primitive root; to bear young; causatively to beget; medically, to act as midwife; spec. to show lineage:— bear, beget, birth ([-day]), born, (make to) forth (children, young), bring up, calve, child, come, be delivered (of a child), time of delivery, gender, hatch, labor, (do the office of a) midwife, declare pedigrees, be the son of, (woman in, woman that) travail (-eth, -ing woman). — *The New Strong's Dictionary of Hebrew and Greek Words*. Nashville: Thomas Nelson, 1996.

CHAPTER 9

REVEALING FALSEHOOD

We need to be learners to be successful disciples (as stated in Chapter 6); students who not only acquire information, but who also strive to be like their teacher. Learning is what will separate us from theology that is not in harmony with God's will.

The centuries of additions to Christian theology have altered the Way as it was known by Jesus and the Apostles. This has led to modern-day Christendom, which is a collection of various flavors of worship and understanding that has hidden many of the truths recognized in the 1st-century. While our salvation is not due to any act on our part, but is entirely a gift from our Creator, how we worship is important. It is the only way we can demonstrate appreciation and honor our heavenly Father. Which is why John wrote the following:

> But an hour is coming—and now is here—when the true worshipers will worship the Father in spirit and truth, for indeed the Father seeks such people to be his worshipers. God is spirit, and the ones who worship him must worship in spirit and truth. - *John 4:23,24 LEB.*

The weeds of non-biblical beliefs have choked the modern

Christian understanding of the word of God. If a belief is not based on the Word of God, it makes our worship invalid from God's perspective, and His perspective is the only one that matters.

The 1st-century Jews were divided into sects. They lived amid multiple denominations of Judaism, each with the basic foundation of the Mosaic Law, but corrupted by man-made assumptions and rules, which is why John recorded the following words of Jesus:

> So Jesus said to the Jews who had believed him, "If you abide in my word, you are truly my disciples, and you will know the truth, and the truth will set you free." — *John 8:31,32 ESV.*

Abiding in Jesus' word will set us free from the assumptions and rules added to scripture by men. This was true for 1st-century Jews, and it is true for us today. While modern Christendom has thousands more denominations than 1st-century Judaism, the corruption is the same; there is no order-of-degrees beyond Yahweh's word. We are either holding fast to his word, or we are not.

> Therefore, I, the prisoner in the Lord, exhort you to live in a manner worthy of the calling with which you were called: with all humility and gentleness, with patience, putting up with one another in love, being eager to keep the unity of the Spirit in the bond of peace; one body and one Spirit (just as also you were called with one hope of your calling), one Lord, one faith, one baptism, one God and Father of all, who is over all, and through all, and in all. — *Ephesians 4:1-6 LEB.*

> Therefore, ridding yourselves of all malice and all deceit and hypocrisy and envy and all slander, like newborn infants long for the unadulterated spiritual milk, so that by it you may grow up to salvation, if you have tasted that the Lord is kind, to whom you are drawing near, a living stone rejected by men but chosen and precious in the sight of God. And you yourselves, as living stones, are being built up as a spiritual house for a holy priesthood, to offer up spiritual sacrifices acceptable to God through Jesus Christ. — *1 Peter 2:1-5 LEB.*

To be part of the spiritual house built on the foundation laid by Jesus, the "living stone rejected by men but chosen and precious in the sight of God," we must shed all worldly attitudes and the mental cages built upon lawless traditions encouraged by Satan.

> You are of your father, the devil, and you want to do the desires of your father. He was a murderer from the beginning, and doesn't stand in the truth, because there is no truth in him. When he speaks a lie, he speaks on his own; for he is a liar, and the father of lies. — *John 8:44 LEB.*

Jesus spoke the above words to the Jews, because they were seeking to kill him (John 8:40). They were sons of the devil, not sons of God. The tradition they added to the Law led them to that position against Jesus.

> Jesus said to them, "If God were your Father, you would love me, for I came from God and I am here. I came not of my own accord, but He sent me. Why do

> you not understand what I say? It is because you cannot bear to hear my word." —*John 8:42,43 ESV.*

That is not a minor offense. The religious tradition the Jews followed blinded them to the truth, and is on par with Adam's refusal to follow Yahweh's guidance. This cannot be stressed enough. Both rejecting or adding to Yahweh's guidance ends with the same result, because both display a lack of integrity toward the Creator, and demonstrate the inner desire to go another way. By doing this, the Pharisees were imitating the Devil, proving they were sons of his way, not Yahweh's.

Many of the religious organizations who claim to be Christian fall short of that expectation. Some, due to strict managerial oversight of the church, have been called cults by outsiders, because of the hold they have on the assembled worshipers. And those worshipers rapidly come and go once they realize the oversight is a man-made burden, similar to the tradition of the Pharisees. While the intent may be well meaning, to better protect people from the influence of the world, all it does is push people away, and cause mental anguish for those who stay.

Hypocrisy is another sign a church is traveling away from the Road to Life.

> A witness of falsehood will not go unpunished, and he who breathes lies will not escape. — *Proverbs 19:5 LEB.*

Hypocrisy can be obvious or it can be subtle. The subtle kind is often hidden by years or centuries of tradition. Because of this, many will not recognize hypocrisy when they hear it. It is hidden from them because it has been held as truth for so long how could it not be true?

There lies the problem (pun intended).

> But as for the cowards and unbelievers and detestable persons and murderers and sexually immoral people and sorcerers and idolaters and all liars, their share is in the lake that burns with fire and sulphur, which is the second death. — *Revelation 21:8 LEB.*

> A faithful witness does not lie, but he who breathes out falsehood is a witness of deceit. — *Proverbs 14:5 LEB.*

The only way to uncover hypocrisy is to acquire knowledge. What we learn must not be concealed in ourselves. It must be said for everyone to hear. People will usually react in one of three ways:

1. Lovers of truth will calmly examine facts, and come to a reasoned conclusion.

2. Lovers of tradition will criticize the new information because it upsets years, or even centuries, of accepted dogma.

3. Others will see the value in the new knowledge, and may even agree with the implications, but they will continue acknowledging the hypocrisy as the correct path for fear of causing upset.

How we react depends on the depth of our conversion. Have we become a "new creation?"

> Therefore, if anyone is in Christ, he is a new creation. The old has passed away; behold, the new has come. — *2 Corinthians 5:17 ESV.*

Are we floundering in the "spirit of the world?"

> Do you not know that friendship with the world is enmity with God? Therefore whoever wishes to be a friend of the world makes himself an enemy of God. Or do you suppose it is to no purpose that the Scripture says, "He yearns jealously over the spirit that he has made to dwell in us?" But he gives more grace. Therefore it says, "God opposes the proud but gives grace to the humble." Submit yourselves therefore to God. Resist the devil, and he will flee from you. — *James 4:1-7 ESV.*

If we are a "new creation," the spirit of God should be our guide.

> Now we have received not the spirit of the world, but the Spirit who is from God, that we might understand the things freely given us by God. — *1 Corinthians 2:12 ESV.*

What Prevents the Removal of Falsehood?

If we are strong with the spirit of God, there is still another hurdle before us: human imperfection.

Rejecting knew ideas is not confined to religion. Many long-standing disciplines in science have been stifled by an unwillingness to adapt to knew data. In Astronomy, the reality of a sun-centered solar system took 1400 years to overcome the mandate of an earth-centered system[1]. The Big Bang Theory, since it's inception, has faced a minimum of thirty scientifically verified results that do not fit the Theory[2]. With the recent James Web Telescope data, Hubble's theory has come under more scrutiny and may finally change.[3] Archeology has also seen push-back against the old theory that the

Clovis People were the oldest settlers in North America.[4]

The sciences are disciplines that change over time due to the discovery of new evidence. Sometimes that change is delayed due to the human insistence for maintaining the status quo. People don't always like change, especially if that change upsets long-standing belief. Some people don't like to be told they are wrong. They can be bound by their belief so much that loosening those bindings leaves them floundering in a new reality they can't understand.

Whether science or religion, we should not let the status quo be the determiner that stifles knowledge. If the data, and corresponding analysis, tell us a different outcome, then our path to the truth should change.

> Let God be true even if every man is a liar. — *Romans 3:4 TCNT*

Chapter Notes

1. Ptolemy's geocentric (Earth-centred) system dominated scientific thought for some 1,400 years. - Britannica Editors. "heliocentrism" Encyclopedia Britannica, December 5, 2025.

https://www.britannica.com/science/heliocentrism.

2. Thomas Van Flandern, *Meta Research Bulletin* 11, p 6-13, 2002 https://www.metaresearch.org/cosmology/cosmology2/the-top-30-problems-with-the-big-bang

3. Eric J. Lerner, President and Chief Scientist of LPPFusion, *The Big Bang Never Happened*, 11th August 2022.

https://iai.tv/articles/the-big-bang-didnt-happen-auid-2215?_auid=2020

Chapter Notes (con.)

[4]. Katherine Harmon, *People Were Chipping Stone Tools in Texas More Than 15,000 Years Ago*, March 24, 2011, Scientific American.

https://www.scientificamerican.com/article/texas-stone-tools-pre-clovis/

CHAPTER 10

BUILDING A FIRM FOUNDATION

A firm foundation is essential for success. This is true of all subjects that require extensive knowledge and time to achieve mastery over the subject matter. A strong foundation to support our faith must be built with knowledge that is harmonious, in agreement with Yahweh's will.

> Everyone who comes to me and hears my words and does them, I will show you what he is like: He is like a man building a house, who dug and went down deep and laid the foundation on the rock. And when a flood came, the river burst against that house and was not able to shake it, because it had been built well. — *Luke 6:47,48 LEB.*

The only foundation that will be successful is the one laid by Yahweh. All others will eventually fail, because they are built upon the shifting sands of misguided theology. If faith is based on human philosophy or influenced by expressions inspired by demons (1 Timothy 4:1), it will crack and crumble under the weight of unfulfilled promises.

Breaking Through Flawed Theology

An example of a strong or weak foundation is how we understand two similar events in scripture: Hebrews 11:5 and 2 Kings 2:11.

Hebrews 11:5

> By faith Enoch was taken up so that he should not see death, and he was not found, because God had taken him. Now before he was taken he was commended as having pleased God. — *Hebrews 11:5 ESV.*

Was Enoch taken up by God and transferred to Heaven to be with God? Many people believe he was transferred to Heaven to be with God. The statement in Hebrews is brief and does not contain much detail. The scripture just says, "he was taken up" so he would "not see death," and that "God had taken him." There are no specifics as to where Enoch was taken. It does not say he was taken to be with God. The statement in Genesis about this event says less than the information in Hebrews:

> And Enoch walked with God, and he was no more, for God took him. — *Genesis 5:24 LEB.*

Genesis mentions Enoch fathered "sons and daughters," and that he was 365 years old when God "took him" (Genesis 5:22,23), but it does not say he died or went to heaven to be with God.

2 Kings 2:11

> Then they were walking, talking as they went. Suddenly a fiery chariot with horses of fire appeared and separated between the two of them. Elijah went up in the storm to the heavens — *2 Kings 2:11 LEB.*

Was Elijah taken up to be with God in heaven? Many people believe he was taken to be with God. While the "fiery chariot" took Elijah "to the heavens," no mention is made about this event taking Elijah to be with God. This event took place during the reign of King Jehoshaphat. Years later, during the time of King Jehoram, Jehoshaphat's son, a letter was sent from Elijah:

> And a letter from Elijah the prophet came to him, saying, "Thus says Yahweh, the God of David your father: 'Because you have not walked in the ways of Jehoshaphat your father or in the ways of Asa, the king of Judah, but have walked in the way of the kings of Israel and have enticed Judah and the inhabitants of Jerusalem to be unfaithful like the unfaithfulness of the house of Ahab, and have also murdered your brothers of the house of your father who were better than you, behold, Yahweh is inflicting a great plague on your people, your children, your wives, and all your possessions, and you yourself will be afflicted with great illness, with sickness in your bowels, until your bowels come out on account of the illness, day by day.'" — *2 Chronicles 21:12-15 LEB.*

To explain the existence of this letter, years after Elijah was taken "into the heavens," most commentators rely on different assumptions to explain the apparent inconsistency.

> **1. Elijah's Letter Was Written Before His Ascension:** Elijah, anticipating Jehoram's future apostasy, composed and dispatched a letter that might have been delivered only after Elijah was taken up.
> **2. Different Ordering of Events:** The narrative of 2 Kings might not align chronologically with the passage in 2 Chronicles. Elijah could still have been on earth by the time of Jehoram's early rule.
> **3. Prophetic Community's Role:** Elijah's successors, such as Elisha or other sons of the prophets, faithfully preserved and carried Elijah's message forward, just as Moses' words were preserved and read long after Moses departed. — *Bible Hub, How did Elijah send a letter post-ascension?* https://biblehub.com/q/how_did_elijah_send_a_letter_post-ascension.htm.

Moving Beyond Speculations

Speculations of this kind are not based on historical data. They are unverified assumptions to support a belief that has no specific biblical foundation. God's proclamations always supersede man's opinions. To understand what happened to Enoch and Elijah, we must consider the context and other statements recorded in scripture.

> Jesus answered and said to him, "Are you the teacher of Israel, and you do not understand these

> things? Truly, truly I say to you, we speak what we know, and we testify about what we have seen, and you do not accept our testimony! If I tell you earthly things and you do not believe, how will you believe if I tell you heavenly things? And no one has ascended into heaven except the one who descended from heaven—the Son of Man. —*John 3:10-12.*

John recorded Jesus' answer to Nicodemus with a direct statement that *"no one has ascended into heaven except the one who descended from heaven."* This is contrary to the idea that Enoch and Elijah ascended into heaven to be with God.

The Greek Word for Heaven

> οὐρανός (*ouranŏs*). Noun, masculine. **Sky.** *The portion of creation that is distinct from earth.*
> This word refers most basically to the part of the universe that cannot be identified as the earth. Thus, Paul can speak of the entire earth with the phrase "all creation under heaven (*ouranŏs*)" (Col 1:23). It is the domain in which clouds hover and birds fly (Matt 26:64; Mark 4:32) as well as the domain where the stars and other heavenly bodies exist (e.g., Mark 13:25). It is also used to describe the realm of transcendent beings in which God dwells on his throne (Rev 4:1–2) and from which Jesus came (1 Cor 15:47). — Jonathon Lookadoo, "Celestial Bodies." In *Lexham Theological Wordbook*, edited by Douglas Mangum, et al, *Lexham Bible Reference Series*. Bellingham, WA: Lexham Press, 2014.

In the Old Testament account of Enoch, the word for heaven is not used. In the account of Elijah, the word for "heavens" is mentioned, and it has a meaning similar to the Greek:

The Hebrew Word for Heaven

> *Šāmayim*; Aram. *šĕmayin;* Noun, masculine, plural. **Sky, heavens.** *The realm in which celestial bodies are located.*
> This Hebrew word for sky is only used in the plural in the Bible. It is the whole region above the earth. This includes the area where meteorological phenomena occur and from which rain falls to the earth (Gen 7:11); it also includes the area in which the celestial bodies are to be found (Gen 1:17). Isaiah (Isa 47:13) condemns those who attempt to determine the future by using astrology to study the sky (*šāmayim*). In accordance with its association with heights, astronomical phenomena, and meteorological events, *šāmayim* came to be known as the place where God was enthroned (Psa 2:4), though God could not be contained even in the heavens (*šāmayim*; 1 Kgs 8:27). The equivalent Aramaic word *šĕmayin* has the same meaning (e.g., Ezra 5:11; Jer 10:11; Dan 7:13). — Jonathon Lookadoo, "Celestial Bodies." In *Lexham Theological Wordbook*, edited by Douglas Mangum, et al, *Lexham Bible Reference Series*. Bellingham, WA: Lexham Press, 2014.

One fact is undeniable: Elijah ascended into the sky. There is no mention of where he was taken or put down, but it is obvious he was still on Earth years later in order to compose and send a letter to King Jehoram. This transfer to another place is similar to what happened to Philip.

> Now an angel of the Lord spoke to Philip, saying, "Get up and go toward the south on the road that goes down from Jerusalem to Gaza." And he got up and went, and behold, there was a man, an Ethiopian eunuch (a court official of Candace, queen of the Ethiopians, who was over all her treasury) who had come to worship in Jerusalem and was returning and sitting in his chariot, and reading aloud the prophet Isaiah.
>
> So Philip . . . heard him reading aloud Isaiah the prophet and said, "So then, do you understand what you are reading?" And he said, "So how could I, unless someone will guide me?" And he invited Philip to come up and sit with him . . . And he ordered the chariot to stop, and they both went down into the water—Philip and the eunuch—and he baptized him. And when they came up out of the water, *the Spirit of the Lord carried Philip away*, and the eunuch did not see him any longer, for he went on his way rejoicing. *But Philip found himself at Azotus*, and as he passed through, he proclaimed the good news to all the towns until he came to Caesarea. — *Acts 8:26-30,31,38-40 LEB (emphasis mine).*

The distance from Gaza to Azotus (also known as Ashdod) is about 30 kilometers (18.6 miles), near the coast, about midway between Joppa and Gaza. The "Spirit of the Lord" carried Philip to

Azotus, and we can infer it was a quick trip because Philip "found himself at Azotus." This transfer to another place by supernatural means is similar to what happened to both Enoch and Elijah, since no one has ascended to be with God, except the one who descended, Jesus the Messiah.

Regarding Enoch, Hebrews 11:5 says, "Enoch was taken up so that he should not see death." This implies that God prevented Enoch from being killed. Enoch lived before the flood, in a violent, lawless world that God later destroyed. This is also speculation, but based on biblical reasoning from what is written, and scriptural support that no man ascended into heaven before Jesus.

No human being could ascend to heaven until after the ransom paid by Jesus. The Messiah's sacrifice covers sin inherited from Adam and allows the dead to be resurrected to a new life, which is the only solution for the sin of Adam. Therefore, no one could ascend to be with God in heaven until after Jesus died and was resurrected (1 Corinthians 15:20, 23).

This understanding of the resurrection was a basic biblical concept in the 1st-century, as explained by Martha:

> So Martha said to Jesus, "Lord, if you had been here, my brother would not have died. Even now I know that whatever you ask God, God will grant you"
> Jesus said to her, "Your brother will rise again."
> Martha said to him, "I know that he will rise again in the resurrection at the last day." — *John 11:21-24 LEB.*

The thought of a resurrection immediately after death was not a biblical concept in the ancient world. Job, who was suffering from terrible physical pain, said this to Yahweh:

> As the waters fail from the sea, and the flood decayeth and drieth up: so man lieth down, and riseth not: till the heavens be no more, they shall not awake, nor be raised out of their sleep. O that thou wouldest hide me in the grave, that thou wouldest keep me secret, until thy wrath be past, that thou wouldest appoint me a set time, and remember me! If a man die, shall he live again? All the days of my appointed time will I wait, till my change come. —*Job 14:11-13 KJV.*

The writer of Hebrews also mentions the limits of our human lives before the sacrifice of the Messiah. Speaking about all the faithful witnesses of God in the past, including Enoch (Hebrews 11:5), he says:

> These all died in faith without receiving the promises, but seeing them from a distance and welcoming them, and admitting that they were strangers and temporary residents on the earth . . . And although they all were approved through their faith, they did not receive what was promised, because God had provided something better for us, so that they would not be made perfect without us. — *Hebrews 11:13,39,40 LEB.*

A reminder in Psalms should always guide our thinking:

> Unless Yahweh builds a house, its builders labor at it in vain. Unless Yahweh guards a city, a guard watches in vain. — *Psalm 127:1 LEB.*

A successful Christian journey will rely on faith based on Yahweh's reality, not the reality influenced by pagan traditions. It will be free of flaws that allow cracks to form, because of assumptions that may seem valid at first, but do not agree with Yahweh's revealed will. To complete our journey, for the Way of Christ to enable us to reach the finish line, we must allow ourselves to be led by the spirit of God and oppose the spirit of the world.

> We know that we are from God, and the whole world lies in the power of the evil one. — *1 John 5:19 LEB.*

> Therefore, as you have received Christ Jesus the Lord, live in him, firmly rooted and built up in him and established in the faith, just as you were taught, abounding with thankfulness. — *Colossians 2:6,7 LEB.*

> For it stands in scripture, "Behold, I am laying in Zion a stone, a chosen and precious cornerstone, and the one who believes in him will never be put to shame." — *1 Peter 2:6 LEB.*

> Now may the God of hope fill you with all joy and peace in believing, so that you may abound in hope by the power of the Holy Spirit. — *Romans 15:13 LEB.*

Chapter 11

Make Sure of All Things

In the last chapter, we saw how statements in isolated scriptures can lead to an understanding that lacks credibility when compared to the larger biblical perspective. This is true in the case of Enoch and Elijah as it is for other beliefs common among modern Christian churches. To remove these types of misconceptions from our understanding, we must apply the following steps to every subject we analyze in the Bible.

Verify Sources: Where does the source of the information get the information? Titles and degrees are fine, but in the end, the evidence presented must be legitimate, not assumption, opinion, or skewed by historical bias. The data should be objective facts.

> All scripture is inspired by God and profitable for teaching, for reproof, for correction, for training in righteousness, in order that the person of God may be competent, equipped for every good work. — *2 Timothy 3:16,17 LEB.*

Cross-Reference Facts: Single statements may give us an impression that is not accurate. Single statements must be harmonious with the entire biblical record.

> As soon as it was night the brothers sent Paul and Silas to Berea. When they arrived, they went to the synagogue of the Jews. Now these Jews were more noble than those in Thessalonica, and they received the word with all eagerness, examining the Scriptures every day to see if what Paul said was true. — *Acts 17:10-11 LEB*

Question Motives: Consider the motives behind the information; who benefits from its acceptance?

> Beware of false prophets who come to you in sheep's clothing, but inside are ravenous wolves. You will recognize them by their fruits: they do not gather grapes from thorn bushes or figs from thistles, do they? In the same way, every good tree produces good fruit, but a bad tree produces bad fruit. A good tree is not able to produce bad fruit, nor a bad tree to produce good fruit. Every tree that does not produce good fruit is cut down and thrown into the fire. As a result, you will recognize them by their fruits. — *Matthew 7:15*-20 LEB.

Engage in critical thinking: apply reasoning and logic to assess validity.

> Dear friends, do not believe every spirit, but test the spirits to determine if they are from God, because many false prophets have gone out into the world. By this you know the Spirit of God: every spirit that confesses Jesus Christ has come in the flesh is from God, and every spirit that does not confess Jesus is

> not from God, and this is the spirit of the antichrist, of which you have heard that it is coming, and now it is already in the world. — *1 John 4:1-3 NET.*

Educate yourself: stay informed on topics of interest to better discern truth from falsehood.

> Now the Spirit explicitly says that in the later times some will desert the faith and occupy themselves with deceiving spirits and demonic teachings, influenced by the hypocrisy of liars whose consciences are seared. — *1 Timothy 4:1,2 GNB.*

> For there will be a time when they will not put up with sound teaching, but in accordance with their own desires, they will accumulate for themselves teachers, because they have an insatiable curiosity, and they will turn away from the hearing of the truth, but will turn to myths. — *2 Timothy 4:3,4 LEB.*

These admonitions to reject falsehood were an immediate concern in the 1st-century. Paul, in his letters, combated views contrary to the original gospel of Jesus as the true Messiah and the sacrificial ransom provided by Yahweh for Adam's lawless offspring. All the apostles and faithful disciples fought to keep the faith clean of apostate ideas.

Some changes slowly crept into the faith because of language limitations, but also because the understanding of God's abilities were altered by the influx of pagan concepts.

The Almighty God Yahweh has limitations, and this is one of the first truths about His nature that was hidden. This is something rarely talked about, but we cannot fully understand Him if we ignore these important aspects of what makes Him Almighty. Here are the limitations of Yahweh:

1. The Almighty God cannot die. This aspect of his existence is made known to us in both the Old and New Testaments. "For with you is the fountain of life," (Psalm 36:9). "Even from everlasting to everlasting, you are God," (Psalm 90:2). "You are from everlasting," (Psalm 93:2). "We cannot fully know his greatness or count the number of his years," (Job 36:26), "But Yahweh is the true God, he is the living God, and an everlasting king," (Jeremiah 10:10). "Now to the King of the ages, immortal, invisible, to the only God, be honor and glory forever and ever. Amen." (1 Timothy 1:17).

2. The Almighty God is incorruptible. Being "incorruptible" (Romans 1:23), means his body cannot decay. He cannot physically degrade to a lower state of existence. He cannot change from spirit to flesh. The Greek word ἄφθαρτος (aphthartŏs), is translated both "incorruptible" and "immortal." (See also 1 Timothy 1:17).

3. The Almighty God cannot be seen by human eyes. Yahweh told Moses, "You are not able to see my face, because a human will not see me and live." (Exodus 33:20).

> This is well explained by Rabbi Jehudah, in Sepher Cosri (P. iv. § 3): "Of that divine glory mentioned in the Scripture, there is one degree which the eyes of the prophets were able to explore; another which all the Israelites saw, as the cloud and consuming fire; the third is so bright, and so dazzling, that no mortal is able to comprehend it; but should anyone venture to look on it, his whole frame would be dissolved." In such inconceivable splendour is the Divine Majesty

> revealed to the inhabitants of the celestial world, where he is said to "dwell in the light which no man can approach unto" (1Ti_6:16). - *Treasury of Scriptural Knowledge*, by Canne, Browne, Blayney, Scott, and others, with introduction by R. A. Torrey. Published in 1834; public domain.

This agrees with Paul's statement: "For indeed our God is a consuming fire," (Hebrews 12:29).

If this is true, how did Yahweh create biological life? Notice Genesis says "*let us* create man in our image, in our likeness" (Genesis 1:26). Yahweh was speaking to other heavenly beings. Heavenly beings He created. We know that angels can materialize in human form and eat and drink with humans (Hebrews 13:2). While God's spirit is called his "fingers" (Psalm 8:3), which is the tool he uses to create things, we also know that he created everything through his Only Begotten Son (1 Corinthians 8:6; Colossians 1:15,16; Hebrews 2:10). This son was the first heavenly being created (he was begotten, the firstborn), who could exist with biological creatures without destroying them, just like an angel can safely eat, drink and be seen by humans. (Genesis 18:2-8; 19:1-3; Judges 13:15-25).

4. The Almighty God does not lie. (1 Kings 17:24; Psalm 119:160; John 17:17; 2 Timothy 2:13; Titus 1:2). This is a primary personality trait that must always be considered when analyzing Yahweh's words and actions.

5. The Almighty God is not evil. (James 1:17; 1 John 4:8; Deuteronomy 32:4; Exodus 34:6; Romans 9:14). A primary trait that impacts Yahweh's justice.

By ignoring these traits of Yahweh, Christianity adopted pagan beliefs contrary to scripture. They split God into different individuals to allow part of him to exist within the human body of Jesus, so "God" could be manifested on the Earth, elevating Christ's position in the eyes of gentile converts. God, not a perfect man equal to Adam, became the sacrifice. This not only ignores scriptures that indicate Yahweh sent his son, (not a manifestation from a pagan multi-person "Godhead"[1]), it ignores Yahweh's perfect justice that demands payment equal to the crime. (Deuteronomy 19:21). The ransom sacrifice was made to cover the sin of Adam, a once perfect man, not the actions of a God, which makes the altered payment unequal to the crime.

The adopted "Godhead" concept fails because it also ignores the Almighty God's incorruptibility; he cannot die. The inability to see God's face was also ignored to allow humans to see God as Jesus, and it ignores that the profound power of the Almighty can never be contained within a human body, because if the heavens cannot contain him (1 Kings 8:27), being embodied as a human is impossible.

> No one has seen God at any time. The one and only Son, who is in the bosom of the Father, he has declared him. —*John 1:18 WEB.*

> And John bore witness: "I saw the Spirit descend from heaven like a dove, and it remained on him. I myself did not know him, but he who sent me to baptize with water said to me, 'He on whom you see the Spirit descend and remain, this is he who baptizes with the Holy Spirit.' And I have seen and

> have borne witness that this is the Son of God." — *John 1:32-34 LEB.*
>
> And the Father who sent me has Himself borne witness about me. His voice you have never heard, his form you have never seen, and you do not have his word abiding in you, for you do not believe the one whom He has sent." —*John 5:37,38 ESV.*
>
> I [Jesus] have revealed your name [Yahweh] to the men whom you gave me out of the world. They were yours, and you have given them to me, and they have kept your word. . . .Just as you sent me into the world, I also have sent them into the world. And for them I sanctify myself, so that they themselves also may be sanctified in the truth. And I do not ask on behalf of these only, but also on behalf of those who believe in me through their word, that they all may be one, just as you, Father, are in me and I am in you, that they also may be in us, in order that the world may believe that you sent me. And the glory that you have given me, I have given to them, in order that they may be one, just as we are one, I in them, and you in me, in order that they may be completed in one, so that the world may know that you sent me, and you have loved me before the foundation of the world. — *John 17:6,18-26 LEB.*

The title "Son of God" is an important identifier. That term never identifies the Almighty God, because Yahweh is a self-existing person who caused the creation of all other beings (Psalm 148:1-5), whether in heaven or on the Earth. A son is always a created being and owes his life to his father. (Luke 3:38). This is why Jesus said, "I live because of the Father," (John 6:57), and "The Father is greater than I am," (John 14:28).

Remember, God's word must be harmonious. There can be no contradictions. Human prophets performed miracles, not because they were God, but because they represented Yahweh and his spirit was directed through them. Jesus was the Christ, the Anointed One, sent to save Adam's offspring from death, and to restore Yahweh's will upon the Earth. He was like Moses, who was anointed to free Abraham's offspring from Egypt. Both men fulfilled their roles. Moses died and was buried. Jesus died and was resurrected as a spirit (1 Corinthians 15: 20-22), and crowned with a superior position in heaven as a reward for his faithfulness to Yahweh's will.

> He [Jesus] humbled himself by becoming obedient to the point of death, that is, death on a cross. Therefore also God [Yahweh] exalted him and graciously granted him the name above every name, so that in the name of Jesus every knee should bow, of those in heaven and of those on earth and of those under the earth, and every tongue confess that Jesus Christ is Lord, to the glory of God [Yahweh] the Father. — *Philippians 2:8-11*

To help us break through the veil of non-Christian understanding, the following chapter will focus on how to rediscover God's will.

Chapter Notes

1. Godhead

The Almighty God is not a member of a multi-person Godhead. This concept has dominated Christian thought only since the 4th and 5th centuries. In the OT, Yahweh is designated a singular being of unmatched glory, who gives to all other beings, life and breath and everything.

> Hear, Israel: Yahweh is our God. Yahweh is one. — *Deuteronomy 6:4 WEB*
>
> One of the scribes came, and heard them questioning together. Knowing that [Jesus] had answered them well, asked him, "Which commandment is the greatest of all?" Jesus answered, "The greatest is 'Hear, Israel, the Lord our God, the Lord is one'"... The scribe said to him, "Truly, teacher, you have said well that he is one, and there is none other but he" . . . When Jesus saw that he answered wisely, he said to him, "You are not far from God's Kingdom." — *Mark 12:28,29,32,34 WEB.*
>
> The God who made the world and all the things in it. This one, being Lord of heaven and earth, does not live in temples made by human hands, nor is he served by human hands as if he needed anything, because he himself gives to everyone life and breath and everything. — *Acts 17:25 LEB*
>
> The trinity of God is defined by the Church as the belief that in God are three persons who subsist in one nature. The belief as so defined was reached only in the 4th and 5th centuries AD and hence is not explicitly and formally a biblical belief. . . The trinitarian definitions arose as a result of long controversies in which these terms and others such as "essence" and "substance" were erroneously applied to God by some theologians. — John L. McKenzie, S.J., *Trinity, Dictionary of the Bible,* Macmillan Publishing Company, 1965, page 899.

The honest revealing of facts about the Trinity by John L. Mackenzie, a Catholic Jesuit priest, should cause all Christians to pause and consider the denial of facts that must occur for people to perpetuate the Trinity lie. Perhaps another reading of Paul's warnings to Timothy will make a difference.

> Now the Spirit explicitly says that in the last times some will depart from the faith, paying attention to deceitful spirits and teachings of demons. — *1 Timothy 4:1 LEB*

> For the time is coming when people will not endure sound teaching, but having itching ears they will accumulate for themselves teachers to suit their own passions, and will turn away from listening to the truth and wander off into myths.
> — *2 Timothy 4:3,4 ESV.*

Chapter 12

Acquiescing to God's Will

Replacing our worldly personality with a Christian personality takes effort and time. Our growth through physical childhood takes years. Our spiritual growth is also a gradual process. The following list encompasses the necessary steps to successfully navigate the Road to Life.

1. Seek Guidance

A journey without a guide will always be a wasted effort. God's word will draw us closer to Yahweh through Jesus Christ, because Jesus is the mediator between God and human beings, and the Christ will lead us to victory.

> For there is one God, and there is one who brings God and human beings together, the man Christ Jesus. — *1 Timothy 2:5 GNB.*

> Trust Yahweh with all your heart; do not lean toward your own understanding. In all your ways acknowledge him, and he will straighten your paths. — *Proverbs 3:5-6 LEB.*

> "For I know the plans that I am planning concerning you," declares Yahweh, "plans for prosperity and not for harm, to give to you a future and a hope." — *Jeremiah 29:11 LEB.*

> I will instruct you and teach you in the way that you should go. I will advise you with my eye upon you. — *Psalms 32:8 LEB.*

> If any of you lacks wisdom, let him ask God, who gives generously to all without reproach, and it will be given him. —*James 1:5 ESV.*

> Do not be conformed to this present world, but be transformed by the renewing of your mind, so that you may test and approve what is the will of God — what is good and well-pleasing and perfect. — *Romans 12:2 NET.*

2. Live with Purpose

For any journey to be successful, our focus must be on the end result, because the end is our motivation, the reason we continue to strive forward.

> For we are his creation, created in Christ Jesus for good works, which God prepared beforehand, so that we may walk in them. — *Ephesians 2:10 LEB.*

> Whatever you are doing, work at it with enthusiasm, as to the Lord and not for people, because you know that you will receive your inheritance from the Lord

as the reward. Serve the Lord Christ. — *Colossians 3:23-24 NET.*

But you are a chosen race, a royal priesthood, a holy nation, a people for God's possession, so that you may proclaim the virtues of the one who called you out of darkness into his marvelous light. — *1 Peter 2:9 LEB.*

And I am sure of this, that he who began a good work in you will bring it to completion at the day of Jesus Christ. — *Philippians 1:6 ESV.*

Before I formed you in the womb I knew you, and before you came out from the womb I consecrated you; I appointed you as a prophet to the nations. — *Jeremiah 1:5 LEB.*

3. Trust in God

We can walk the road to life with confidence, because Yahweh is faithful. What he says will always prove to be true, and he has sent his only Son to be our guide, who will never lead us astray.

For everything there is an appointed time, a time for every matter under heaven. — *Ecclesiastes 3:1 LEB.*

Wait for Yahweh. Be strong and let your heart show strength, and wait for Yahweh. — *Psalm 27:14 LEB.*

But those who wait for Yahweh shall renew their strength. They shall go up with wings like eagles; they

> shall run and not grow weary; they shall walk and not be faint. — *Isaiah 40:31 LEB.*

> For still the vision awaits its appointed time; it hastens to the end—it will not lie. If it seems slow, wait for it; it will surely come; it will not delay. — *Habakkuk 2:3 ESV.*

> Commit to Yahweh your way; Trust also on him and he will act. Then he will bring forth your righteousness like the light, and your justice like the noonday. — *Psalm 37:5,6 LEB.*

4. Be Willing to Change

A journey needs preparation before it begins, and continual replenishment of supplies along the way if we hope to reach our goal. This may demand changes to our path, and changes to ourselves, but with persistent effort we will not fail.

> I am able to do all things by the one who strengthens me. — *Philippians 4:13 LEB.*

> Behold, I am doing a new thing; now it springs forth, do you not perceive it? I will make a way in the wilderness and rivers in the desert. — *Isaiah 43:19 ESV.*

> So then, if anyone is in Christ, he is a new creation; what is old has passed away — look, what is new has come! — *2 Corinthians 5:17 NET.*

> And we know that all things work together for good for those who love God, who are called according to his purpose. — *Romans 8:28 NET.*

> And he said to them, "Follow me and I will make you fishers of people." — *Matthew 4:19 LEB.*

5. Serve Others

Our roadway will have many obstacles. We will encounter others along our journey who need help. Our service to others will be repaid to us when the need arises. God never forsakes those who love his people.

> For you were called to freedom, brothers. Only do not let your freedom become an opportunity for the flesh, but through love serve one another. For the whole law is fulfilled in one statement, namely, "You shall love your neighbor as yourself." — *Galatians 5:13, 14 LEB,*

> For even the Son of Man did not come to be served, but to serve, and to give his life as a ransom for many. — *Mark 10:45 LEB.*

> Just as each one has received a gift, use it for serving one another, as good stewards of the varied grace of God. — *1 Peter 4:10 LEB.*

> For God is not unjust, so as to forget your work and the love which you demonstrated for his name by

> having served the saints, and continuing to serve them. — *Hebrews 6:10 LEB.*

> And the king will answer *and* say to them, "Truly I say to you, in as much as you did it to one of the least of these brothers of mine, you did it to me." — *Matthew 25:40 LEB.*

6. Endure Trials

Hardships of many kinds can strike at any moment on our Road to Life, because time and unforeseen occurrences happen to all mankind. We need endurance to travel along the Road to Life.

> Again, I observed this on the earth: the race is not always won by the swiftest, the battle is not always won by the strongest; prosperity does not always belong to those who are the wisest, wealth does not always belong to those who are the most discerning, nor does success always come to those with the most knowledge — for time and chance may overcome them all. — *Ecclesiastes 9:11 NET.*

> My brothers and sisters, consider it nothing but joy when you fall into all sorts of trials, because you know that the testing of your faith produces endurance. And let endurance have its perfect effect, so that you will be perfect and complete, not deficient in anything. — *James 1:2-4 NET.*

> Not only this, but we also rejoice in sufferings, knowing that suffering produces endurance, and

endurance, character, and character, hope. — *Romans 5:3-4 NET.*

I have fought the good fight, I have completed the race, I have kept the faith. — *2 Timothy 4:7 NET.*

Although now for a short time, if necessary, you are distressed by various trials, so that the genuineness of your faith, more valuable than gold that is passing away, but is tested by fire, may be found to result in praise and glory and honor at the revelation of Jesus Christ. — *1 Peter 1:6-7 LEB.*

Therefore, since we also have such a great cloud of witnesses surrounding us, putting aside every weight and the sin that so easily ensnares us, let us run with patient endurance the race that has been set before us, fixing our eyes on Jesus, the originator and perfecter of faith, who for the joy that was set before him endured the cross, disregarding the shame, and has sat down at the right hand of the throne of God. — *Hebrews 12:1-2 LEB.*

7. Be Content

Satisfaction comes from appreciation. Our appreciation comes from the realization of our place in God's Kingdom. Our journey on the Road to Life is not just for our benefit, it is for the benefit of all of Yahweh's creation. It is a journey that will never see regret.

Not that I speak from need, for I have learned to be content in whatever circumstances I am. I know how both to make do with little and I know how to have an abundance. In everything and in all things I have learned the secret both to be filled and to be hungry, both to have an abundance and to go without. I am able to do all things by the one who strengthens me. — *Philippians 4:11-12 LEB.*

But godliness with contentment is a great means of gain. For we have brought nothing into the world, so that neither can we bring anything out. But if we have food and clothing, with these things we will be content. — *1 Timothy 6:6-8 LEB.*

Take pleasure in Yahweh as well, and he will give to you the requests of your heart. — *Psalms 37:4 LEB.*

Your lifestyle must be free from the love of money, being content with what you have. For he himself has said, "I will never desert you, and I will never abandon you." — *Hebrews 13:5 LEB.*

Therefore do not be anxious, saying, "What will we eat?" or "What will we drink?" or "What will we wear?" for the pagans seek after all these things. For your heavenly Father knows that you need all these things. But seek first his kingdom and righteousness, and all these things will be added to you. — *Matthew 6:31-33 LEB.*

Chapter 13

The Life Worth Living

Adam and Eve shared a unique perspective. The heavenly being called the Satan and the Devil also had a unique perspective. They all sought immediate gratification. They wanted to advance their positions by sidestepping the Creator. They lacked patience.

> At its core, patience is the capacity to tolerate delay, discomfort, or frustration without losing your sense of direction. That makes it more than good manners. It becomes a skill tied to self-control, emotional balance, and long-term thinking. — *Susan Anderson, Cottonwood Psychology, 2026, https://cottonwoodpsychology.com/.*

> Better is the end of a thing than its beginning, and the patient in spirit is better than the proud in spirit. — *Ecclesiastes 7:8 LEB.*

Adam's, Eve's, and Satan's viewpoints promoted independence, a do-it-yourself attitude, not reliant on their Creator. While there is nothing wrong with wanting to accomplish something on our own, if we ignore the boundaries set by our Creator, our lives will end up with major complications.

> Fools rush in where angels fear to tread. —*Alexander Pope, 1711, An Essay on Criticism.*

For Adam, Eve, and the Satan, that major complication was eternal destruction. For some, eternal destruction may seem like an exaggerated response for wanting to pursue a life not sanctioned by God. That was the Satan's argument, and is still his primary focus as he strives to prove his allegations against Yahweh are justified. But there is more involved than just some personal preference in how things should be done.

Yahweh, the Creator, is the source of everything that exists in our universe and in the spiritual realm where angels reside. He is the sole individual who designed and supplied the material for everything that was made, and established the rules that govern how everything functions and fits together. He is the only self-existent being who resides outside all created things. The heavens cannot contain him (2 Chronicles 6:18). He knows how everything began and how everything will end (Revelation 1:8). His knowledge and wisdom are far beyond the intellect of anyone who was made (Proverbs 2:6; Romans 11:33). His status as the Creator places him in a position that can never be revoked. He is the sovereign ruler of His kingdom, and His kingdom authority encompasses everything that has been made. There is no place beyond the reach of his kingdom. His law is the only legitimate law, and overrides all other laws. (Psalm 145:13).

> "Remember this and stand firm, recall it to mind, you transgressors, remember the former things of old; for I am God, and there is no other; I am God, and there

> is none like me, declaring the end from the beginning and from ancient times things not yet done, saying, 'My counsel shall stand, and I will accomplish all my purpose.'" — *Isaiah 46:8-10 ESV.*

By rejecting Yahweh's authority, we tell him we choose not to live by his standards. If we do not live by his standards, there is no place for us in His kingdom. Since His kingdom encompasses everything made, there is no longer a place for us to exist. The only possible result for the decision to reject Yahweh's guidance is eternal destruction.

> This is evidence of the righteous judgment of God, that you may be considered worthy of the kingdom of God, for which you are also suffering — since indeed God considers it just to repay with affliction those who afflict you, and to grant relief to you who are afflicted as well as to us, when the Lord Jesus is revealed from heaven with his mighty angels in flaming fire, inflicting vengeance on those who do not know God and on those who do not obey the gospel of our Lord Jesus. They will suffer the punishment of eternal destruction, away from the presence of the Lord and from the glory of his might. — *2 Thessalonians 1:5-9 ESV.*

We can also be thankful that Yahweh, our Eternal Creator, is humble.

> King David wrote: "You [Yahweh] also gave me the shield of your salvation, and your right hand

> supported me, and your humility made me great." — *Psalm 18:35 LEB.*

Yahweh's humble nature allows his intelligent creations to accomplish things on their own, within the boundaries of his guidance (See 2 Chronicles 18:19-21). He allowed David to be King of Israel (a position rightfully held by Yahweh). He allows all beings who reflect his image to have free will. He wants those who serve him to do so because they want to serve him, not because he demands it. And he has made a way for Adam's lawless offspring to be adopted back into his universal family and reap the benefits of His kingdom.

> And you, although you were dead in your trespasses and sins, in which you formerly walked according to the course of this world, according to the ruler of the authority of the air, the spirit now working in the sons of disobedience, among whom also we all formerly lived in the desires of our flesh, doing the will of the flesh and of the mind, and we were children of wrath by nature, as also the rest of them were.
>
> But God, being rich in mercy, because of his great love with which he loved us, and we being dead in trespasses, he made us alive together with Christ (by grace you are saved), and raised us together and seated us together in the heavenly places in Christ Jesus, in order that he might show in the coming ages the surpassing riches of his grace in kindness upon us in Christ Jesus.
>
> For by grace you are saved through faith, and this is not from yourselves, it is the gift of God; it is not

> from works, so that no one can boast. For we are his creation, created in Christ Jesus for good works, which God prepared beforehand, so that we may walk in them. — *Ephesians 2: 1-10 LEB.*

Yahweh is willing to overlook our lawless existence if our faith in the ransom of his Only Begotten Son is sincere and knowable by the changing of our perspective toward our place in the present world. With our minds made over by rejecting the spirit of the world, we place ourselves under the guidance of Jesus, the Messiah who gave his life for Adam's offspring, to build up the house of Yahweh and fulfill the purpose of creation.

> But the fruit of the Spirit is love, joy, peace, patience, kindness, goodness, faithfulness, gentleness, self-control. Against such things there is no law. — *Galatians 5:22,23 LEB.*

> Consider it all joy, my brothers, whenever you encounter various trials, because you know that the testing of your faith produces endurance. And let endurance have its perfect effect, so that you may be mature and complete, lacking in nothing. — *James 1:3,4 LEB.*

> Therefore, as the chosen of God, holy and dearly loved, put on affection, compassion, kindness, humility, gentleness, patience, putting up with one another and forgiving one another. If anyone should have a complaint against anyone, just as also the Lord

forgave you, thus also you do the same. — *Colossians 3:12,13 LEB.*

Love must be without hypocrisy. Abhor what is evil; be attached to what is good, being devoted to one another in brotherly love, esteeming one another more highly in honor, not lagging in diligence, being enthusiastic in spirit, serving the Lord, rejoicing in hope, enduring in affliction, being devoted to prayer. — *Romans 12:12 LEB.*

And let us not grow weary in doing good, for at the proper time we will reap, if we do not give up. — *Galatians 6:9 LEB.*

But if we hope for what we do not see, we await it eagerly with patient endurance. — *Romans 8:25 LEB.*

Be quiet before Yahweh and wait for him. Do not fret about one who succeeds in his way, about a man making plots. Refrain from anger and forsake wrath. Do not fret; it only brings evil. For evildoers will be cut off, but those who wait for Yahweh—they will possess the land. — *Psalm 37:7-9 LEB.*

"For I know the plans that I am planning concerning you," declares Yahweh, "plans for prosperity and not for harm, to give to you a future and a hope." — *Jeremiah 29:11 LEB.*

Scripture Index

Scripture Index

Scripture Index

Scripture Index

OTHER THEOCRATIC BOOKS BY P.D. BLACKWELL

Lawless Tradition:
God's Victory Despite Christendom's Failure
https://www.amazon.com/dp/1736609637

PRAISE FOR LAWLESS TRADITION

Lawless Tradition is a tour de force with an engaging literary style that educates the reader along the journey.

— Kimberly Vargas, *Award Wining Author*

Lawless Tradition is a book of divine wisdom, understanding, and discovery. A guide to help true Christians better understand God.

— Anthionette Ejimofor, *Goodreads.com*

The amount of study and preparation put into this work is evident and instills in the reader a fair amount of confidence in the authenticity of this book. Nothing is pulled out of thin air; everything is backed up with evidence.

— Nzube Chizoba Okeke, *Online Book Club .Org*

This is a solid book with so much scriptural backing and commentary from theologians to support its interpretations that it cannot be reasonably ignored. Very highly recommended.

— Asher Syed, *Reader's Favorite*

P. D. Blackwell takes a deep dive into word meanings and cultural context . . . Explaining in easy-to-understand terms how to develop a first century understanding, Blackwell leads to a logical conclusion.

— Philip Van Heusen, *Reader's Favorite*

SCIENCE FICTION BOOKS BY P.D. BLACKWELL

Chaos Rising:
The Erstallius Chronicles, Volume One
https://www.amazon.com/dp/B08W9RJ6K6

PRAISE FOR CHAOS RISING

A compelling, complex, and cinematic work of science fiction with plenty of chilling psychological undertones and all-out action scenes.
— K.C. Finn, *Reader's Favorite.*

If you enjoy complex, well-developed science fiction novels, you'll want to check out Blackwell's book. I loved how this adventure takes the reader to many new destinations full of diverse cultures, vivid landscapes, and honored pasts.
— Erin Dydek, *Online Book Club. Org.*

Blackwell excels at characterization and vivid portrayals of each scene. Chaos Rising is edgy, clever, and layered. It kept me glued to its pages.
— Lit Amiri, *Reader's Favorite.*

It was well-written and I enjoyed how the story flowed smoothly at a good pace. The characters in the story were strong, complex and likeable, and I truly rooted for them from beginning to end.
— Leah Gonzalez, *Reader's Favorite.*

SCIENCE FICTION BOOKS BY P.D. BLACKWELL

The Rhysu Alternative,
The Erstallius Chronicles, Volume Two
https://www.amazon.com/dp/B08W8QTC9

PRAISE FOR THE RHYSU ALTERNATIVE

I already had high expectations before starting The Rhysu Alternative. I was expecting the same level of intricate plot, smart characters, and impressive narrative. I was completely surprised when P.D. Blackwell exceeded all of my expectations and gave me a lot more.

— Rabia Tanveer, *Reader's Favorite.*

Author P. D. Blackwell presents a worthy sequel after the excellent worldbuilding and complex emotional dynamics of the first foray into this incredible universe. After what Bev went through in the opening novel, I thought it would be hard to top, but her journey of empowerment in her new situation was really inspiring.

— K.C. Finn, *Reader's Favorite.*

Blackwell creates conflict at multiple levels without taking away from the story the balance it deserves. The crisp prose is enriched by the engaging dialogues, but the strength of the narrative lies in the author's expert handling of plot points and the conflict which escalates to an explosive climax.

— Romuald Dzemo, *Reader's Favorite*

ABOUT THE AUTHOR:

P.D. Blackwell is a lifelong student who began studying theology, religion, and physics in 1980. He practices the guitar everyday, and enjoys a good game of chess.

www.ingramcontent.com/pod-product-compliance
Lightning Source LLC
LaVergne TN
LVHW091002080826
845145LV00003B/1099

* 9 7 8 1 7 3 6 6 0 9 6 5 1 *